ONE RAUCOUS LOVE SONG

POEMS OF WONDER AND HOPE

KARYN HENLEY

ANDON PRESS

NASHVILLE

One Raucous Love Song, Poems of Wonder and Hope

www.KarynHenley.com

ISBN 979-8-9870550-2-1(pbk), 979-8-9870550-3-8 (epub)

Contents

Let Time Tumble	1
Flickering Flame	2
Full of the Secret	3
Winter Garden	4
Absolutely Nothing	6
Go Open the Door	8
A Gentle, Ancient Heartbeat	9
Waking to Snow	10
Watching Planes	11
The In-Between Times	13
Open-Eyed and Full-Hearted	15
Around an Unfrozen Pool	16
Something About the Night	18
Delight in This Day	19
We Bring Things	20
The Joy in Waiting	21
A Whisper of Spring	23
For a Day Born New	24
A Perplexed Rose	25
Slowing Down with the Rain	26

It Came as a Question   28

Magical Moon   30

At the Tail End of Winter   32

A Private Nod   33

From the Hospital Window   35

The Wonder-Work of Winter   37

A Backyard Chorus Line   39

The Sun Yawned   41

Caught by Surprise   42

I Imagined Fog Drifting In   44

Roof Ornament   46

Except for the Violets   47

Painted with Joy   49

Not the Off-Hand "Thanks"   50

Growing Up With the Wind   51

At the Edge of My Coffee   53

Looking Up   54

I Saw You   55

And Still They Come   56

Butterfly   57

The Deep Knowing of a Stone   58

Slipped Between the Pages	59
If I Take the Hint	61
The Thinnest of Tightropes	62
The Song of All-is-Done	64
What the Bee Sees	66
What if You Were the Wind?	68
I Know Nothing	70
So Many Reasons	72
One of These Days	74
Afraid I Might Fall	75
Bluebird Between Storms	76
Ah, the Dahlia	78
The Bell Tower	80
A Game of War I Don't Want to Play	82
The Moon was Half	83
A Gardener's Optical Illusion	84
The Thread Connecting Us	85
A Gift of Poppies	87
No Hurry, No Worry	89
Where Does the Music Go?	91
Peace, They Insist	93

What the Chipmunk Told Me	95
The Magic of the Ordinary	97
The Word that Waved	99
Perching on My Roof	101
I Spy	102
Silent Green Tongues and Blushing Petals	104
One Glance	105
With a Flash of Wings	107
The Gift of Permission	109
Coneflower Shadow	110
Why I Need My Garden	111
Why Not Love a Tree?	113
Looking at Green	115
Steady and Soft, Damaging and Deadly	117
Look What I Found	119
Until Peace Settles Deeply	121
Swallowing Sunshine	123
Night Has Not Fallen	124
Never Ever Before	125
The Key	126
Could it Become a Symphony?	127

Silenced by the Sea in the Wind 129

A Pure Stream of Blue 130

What If? 131

The Sacrament of Waking 132

Who Knew? 133

Every Drenched Thing 135

A Rather Large Keepsake 136

Playful Day 138

A Silent Slant of Light 139

Simply to be Present 140

The Geese Come Flying Low 141

The Salty Spray of Memory 142

A Waterfall of Music 144

The Invitation and Promise of Earth 145

Splashes in the Birdbath 146

The Color of Life 147

The Wisdom of the Ink 149

Petal by Fascinating Petal 150

Singing in the Storm 151

Some Faithful Thing 152

The Peace of Baking Bread 154

Wishing I Could Fly	155
Home	156
November Marigold	157
Life's Secret Answer	158
Risking It All	160
The Writing Class	162
In the Realm of Inner Peace	164
Held Between	165
Feed Me	166
Center Stage	167
When Dawn Raised Her Window Shade	168
The Dance of the Season	169
When Life Calls You Back in Time	171
One Raucous Love Song	172
Making Waves	173
Morning Gold, Silent as Breath	174
That House is Empty Now	175
Hanging On	177
Having the Maybes	178
Flames of Spring Green	179
Winter and the Wild	180

Lasting the Winter   181

What the Wind Said   183

Winter Evenings   185

On Icy Tiptoe   186

The Contours of the Seasons   187

Winter's Brittle Beauty   188

The Changing Weather of Peace   189

What's the Hurry?   190

Bowing Pines, Drifting Clouds,
and the Scent of Rain   191

Let Time Tumble

Time tumbled through year-end,
and here I am in crisp January,
wrapped in a warm shawl,
sipping decaf coffee,
listening to rain tap against the window,
slowing down,
breathing deep,
beginning again,
hoping I'm wiser this year,
suspecting I'm not,
resolving to give myself grace to grow,
though my grandson would say
that I'm already grown.
And yes, I am.
But no, I'm not.
I know far less now
than when I was young.
I am full of
questions
that will never be answered,
wishes
that will never come true,
uncertainties
that will never resolve.
But here I am in crisp January,
wrapped in a warm shawl,
sipping decaf coffee,
perfectly content just to be
and to let time tumble on.

Flickering Flame

On a gray-white rock
there sits a clear glass cup
that holds a candle
with a flickering flame.
It reminds me of the fire
in the fireplace of the house
where I grew up
and where my father still lives.
At 95 rich, deep years,
he spends most of his time dozing
in a favorite recliner
surrounded by soft pillows.
But when he wakes,
there's the faithful fire
dancing for him,
warming his spirits,
cheering his reveries.
He can turn the flames off
with a remote—
it's a gas fire—
but he leaves it on
all the time,
even in the heat of summer.
The fire is a constant comfort to him.
I will miss that fire
when it goes out.

Full of the Secret

Plump and round, brightly white,
the full moon smiles down
through my window.
I smile back,
for I am also full—
full of peace veiled in soft moonglow,
full, too, of the secret we share,
the moon and I.
Maybe you share the secret too,
the secret of flipping the view.
Imagine the wonder of witnessing,
through a space-traveler's eyes,
the turn-about's-fair-play way
of gazing not at the moon
but at Earth,
of seeing not moonglow
but earthshine.
That is the secret:
the earth glows
just as the moon does.
Moonbeams drift down to Earth,
earthbeams drift up to the moon.
Full moon smiles down,
full Earth smiles up.
And the best part of the secret?
Maybe you didn't know that you glow,
but you do, Earthling,
you do.

Winter Garden

The winter garden is skeletal,
stripped to its bark-bones
and skinny stems.
Brown, brittle seed heads
of Black-eyed Susans shiver
at the wind's cold whisper.
Tattered leaves
of frostbitten Citronella
droop,
dangle,
shudder,
tangle.
A chill gust whips
the dry rust-red cascade
of sleeping Creeping Jenny
into a wide awake, wild dance,
its fronds a frenzy
of airborne ribbons.
Branches of Crape Myrtle sway
like arms with curled fingers
offering pearled brown seed pods
to the winter-blue sky.
If it seems that I'm describing dreariness
and dearth
and death,
perhaps I am.
But I mean to paint a graceful picture,
artful wonders formed by frost
and darkness
and biting wind,
paring back the backyard world
to its simple glory,

its skeletal scaffolding,
the elemental beauty
of Nature's underpainting,
a delicate design
visible only
in this
season.

Absolutely Nothing

So . . . I did nothing,
absolutely nothing
except sit in an easy chair where
I could see out the window.
I did nothing but watch
the sun cross the hardwood floor,
making golden puddles and
shifting the shadows
until lines angled
in a grid of windowpane parallelograms
with long diagonals pointing toward me
or perhaps the reverse,
pointing away from me.
I did absolutely nothing
but watch dust motes drift in a flock
through a broad sunbeam
and think of how we breathe them in and out
all the time.
No doubt they are even now floating
on my out-breath.
Still, I did absolutely nothing
but listen to the Golden bark next door
until she was satisfied that whatever
she was barking at—or for—was
settled.
I did nothing but admire
how the sun glinted through the tips
of my cat's fur,
outlining her back with white light.
Yes, I did absolutely nothing,
for, after all, this is the season of Lent,
and I have decided to fast

from frantic busy-ness.
Plus, my New Year's resolution was
to reclaim one day a week
as a day of rest.
So all afternoon, I sat
in my easy chair
in the sun
with a view out the window.
I did absolutely nothing
and discovered that nothing
is really
Something.

Go Open the Door

Go and open the door.
Maybe outside there is a breeze
that will kiss you
with a sweet scent
or the warm aroma
of a neighbor's fire pit.

Go and open the door.
Maybe a leaf—
the kind that is multi-colored—
will flutter to your feet,
a message of loss that is beautiful anyway,
that carries the hope of springtime
after a long winter of chill weather.

Go and open the door.
Maybe you'll feel the lovingkindness
of the universe.

A Gentle, Ancient Heartbeat

I've said it before,
but I'm growing old,
so I get to say it again:
I love to listen to the quiet.
When I listen to the quiet,
I realize it's not quiet at all.
It's not empty,
it's full,
thrumming,
pulsing,
breathing,
the gentle, ancient heartbeat
of life,
of time,
perhaps of the universe itself.
It's buoyant, this quiet,
full of energy—
a calm forever energy
holding,
enfolding us all.
Shhh.
Pause,
linger,
listen.
Listen
to the quiet.

Waking to Snow

Waking to snow,
deep quiet
feathered flakes,
whispers of wind,
and no one going anywhere.
Time pauses,
takes a break.
Why was I rushing around
all these days past?
What was the hurry, the worry?
Plans have now shifted,
busy has been put on hold.
My old clock softly ticks,
keeping time.
Really, dear clock?
Keeping time?
You keep it only long enough to measure its
passing,
and before you can tick again, it's
gone.
And yet, this morning,
time is asking to be kept,
held,
witnessed
in this white cocoon,
this quiet tiptoe of a morning
waking to snow.

Watching Planes

From where I sit in my after-dinner chair
as sunset dims into twilight,
I can watch airplanes approach
the end of their journey
from the west—
from Dallas
or Denver
or Los Angeles.
Their bright landing lights
cross the darkening sky,
winking in and out of sight
as they thread their way
among silhouettes of tree branches.
By the time one plane
passes overhead with a low hum,
another appears in the distance,
trailing the path of the first one.
Another plane follows.
And another.
Evenly spaced,
they glide smoothly on
like wandering stars.
When I first noticed them,
I thought they truly were stars.
But these stars that are not stars
are full of people
hurtling across the heavens.
These planes I watch,
these travelers
near the end of their journey,
are at the beginning as well.
For what is the end of the journey

but an arrival,
sometimes to a new place,
sometimes home to familiar comforts.
And I wonder:
When I get to the end
of that larger,
longer
journey,
will anyone be watching?
Will I appear as a bright star
slipping through
the night sky,
coming closer and closer?
I have a feeling that for me,
it will feel like coming home.

The In-Between Times

I woke to birdsong this morning,
a good-morning melody
welcoming the silver-gray light
weaving through the clouds and soft rain
of these in-between days
that bridge winter and spring
and seem so random—
today frosty, possible snow,
tomorrow warm, a hug of sunshine.
New blooms have appeared
on the neighbor's hellebore,
Lenten roses right on time.
Purple crocuses have smiled open
under the magnolia,
a bit of yellow peeks from a drift of daffodils
under the hackberry,
all cheering me
in these between times.
And truly, we are always in between—
between starting and finishing,
between losing and finding,
between our last step and our next step.
Isn't it the same with people as with nature?
There are those who bloom
in the in-between times,
those who are our crocuses,
our daffodils,
our Lenten roses,
whose mere presence is a sign of hope,
good cheer,
encouragement
in between the loss of what was

and the uncertainty of what will be,
those who ground us in the present moment
of the in-between.
Thank God for our crocuses,
our daffodils,
our Lenten roses.
Thank God for our in-between friends.

Open-Eyed and Full-Hearted

Sometimes all you can do is
hope
that this year will be better.
I've long passed the stage of
buying into Jiminy Cricket's
"If you wish upon a star…"
I'm way past believing
pie-in-the-sky.
I'm beyond thinking that
if I just do everything right,
everything will be all right.
I'm way past all that.
But I'm not past hope.
I'm not past looking the world
full in the face,
eyes open wide,
and knowing life can be better,
even great,
because
I know people who care.
I know love and peace and joy.
I know kindness and goodness
and grace and generosity.
I'm way past closed eyes
and grasping at straws,
but I'm not past hope.
May we never be past
open-eyed
full-hearted
hope.

Around an Unfrozen Pool

I woke to a world draped in winter white
thicker than a down-filled comforter,
deep enough to swallow my snow boots
up to their necks.
"The fun stuff," said the weatherman,
perfect for building snow people, snow forts,
and snowballs to launch at them.
It wasn't our first snow of the season.
The first snow came several weeks ago
in a light layer falling as I drove home.
Sparkles fluttered past the gleam of headlights
as if God were sprinkling glitter over the city
to celebrate Winter.
By the next morning,
snow-glitter veiled roofs and decks,
grass-blades bent, ice-frosted,
brittle petals shivered, frozen.
Robins gathered at my heated birdbath
like office workers around a water cooler.
Feathers fluffed, bellies round as balls,
they chipped and chirped,
dipped their beaks, bobbed up,
eyed each other.
Until a squirrel came to drink.
Then they flew off together,
all but one brave robin who perched on the porch rail,
squinting over his feathered shoulder,
his back to the squirrel.
When at last the squirrel scampered off,
a mockingbird took its place,
then a cedar waxwing found his way,
maybe straying from his flock,

maybe the only one to spy
and wisely fly
to an unfrozen pool.
The squinting robin finally flew,
but probably just to wait in the nearest tree.
Robins share when they have to,
but I think that they think
they own this spot.
And in a world of winter white,
I am content to let them think so.

Something About the Night

There is something soft and friendly
about the night,
a slowing,
settling,
deep drift
that creeps silently over the world
as the light folds her brightly colored fan
and fades.
Evening shadows gently wash over
grasses and gardens,
chipmunks and squirrels,
bugs and birds.
Darkness rises to the rooftops,
shoulders over the trees
until all rests under a dome of darkness
where stars sail and the moon smiles
and the night breeze dances.
When I was young,
I was taught about heaven.
"There is no night there," we sang,
which saddened me for years.
No night?
No beautiful, calming, restful night?
No chirp of crickets?
No whirr of night bugs?
No lovely call of a lone owl?
I am not convinced about heaven,
but I know the night.
I love the night.
There is something soft and friendly
about the night.

Delight in This Day

Spring danced her way into winter today,
slow twirl of skirts,
whispered breath,
face to the sun.
The birds joined her,
singing Spring,
announcing her presence,
encircling her scent.
Delight in this day, they sing.
Now is the time,
for when Winter finds
that Spring has stepped into his timeline,
he will blow and blast and send her away,
insistent on taking back his season.
But for this day, this moment,
dear Spring,
you are here,
and I will dance with you.

We Bring Things

We bring things for our people—
armfuls of leaves and petals and stems.
We bring things for our people—
paints of red and daffodil yellow,
sea blue and forest green,
poems of peace
and questions for musing.
With outstretched hands,
we bring ourselves—
our seeking souls
our open hearts.
We bring things for our people,
and it's like bringing the sunshine.

I wrote "We Bring Things" thinking about being a facilitator/teacher at Art & Soul Nashville, a community of intuitive artmaking where I take classes and sometimes teach. Who are your people? What do you bring them? What do they bring you? In what communities or friendships do you find peace? Count yourself blessed.

The Joy in Waiting

My backyard neighbor is building a house
at the back corner of his yard.
It's smaller than an apartment,
larger than a tool shed.
He climbs, bends,
measures, hammers.
Slowly it's taking shape,
walls framed,
roof beams pitched just so,
a glass door on the far side,
windows all around,
lots of windows.
Is it a greenhouse?
A woodworking shop?
An office for himself
or his wife?
Maybe in his retirement,
he has taken up painting
or sculpting.
Maybe this is his studio.
I could ask,
but I think the joy will be in waiting,
wondering,
seeing how it turns out.
I once told a watercolor teacher
that I was disappointed in my painting
because it hadn't turned out
the way I had envisioned.
She said, "If it turned out
the way you thought it would,
what's the point?"
Ah.

The point is in the process,
in the trying,
in the discovery.
Still, I know my neighbor has a plan,
and I hope what he's building
will turn out the way he wants.
As for me,
I'll wait and see.

A Whisper of Spring

March, so the saying goes,
comes in like a lion,
out like a lamb.
But it was February that left
roaring,
all in a rush of wind and rain
leaving deck chairs toppled,
branches snapped,
daffodils bowed,
twigs scattered across the lawn.
February was in a hurry
to leave,
and lamb-like,
March has tiptoed in
with silver-gray clouds,
a shy sun
and a spritz of bright yellow forsythia.
Winter has thinned,
and a full-bodied Spring is
peeping in,
seeping in,
reaching out
to hug the world with warmth.
Winter will have a few last words,
but Spring is whispering her arrival,
and I'm listening,
watching,
catching her scent,
feeling her breezy touch.
Hello, March.

For a Day Born New

Good morning, bird,
perched
somewhere outside my open window.
The breeze is carrying your tune
to my drowsy, waking ears.
How long have you been singing
your wake-up song?
Are you a bluebird?
A wren?
A cardinal?
I am not attuned to the differences—
not yet.
No matter.
You are a consummate singer
of carefree song,
melody for a day born new.
The gift of your music
invites me to rise
and breathe deeply of dawn.
Perhaps I, too, will sing.

A Perplexed Rose

I suspect she carried more,
cared more
than I ever knew,
for I never really knew
her.
Irises were her favorites,
but Mother was more like
a rose,
opening slowly,
cautiously,
unsure,
perplexed by layers of petals,
trying to settle them
just
exactly
right
but ending up windblown,
sun-faded,
pollen dusted,
stemmed with thorns,
holding deep in her center
the longing to
do
everything
right
to be the chosen rose.
I think I understand better now,
for I carry more
and care more
than my children will ever know.
Irises are one of my favorites,
but maybe I am a
slowly
unfolding
rose.

Slowing Down with the Rain

The rain did not blow in
the way it often does.
It came straight down
in threads of silver barely visible
against the backdrop of trees.
But I can hear the gentle wash of it
like a stream running over rocks.
It matches my mood—
serene, soft, pensive,
at the shallow end of sadness.
A nuthatch flits from the feeder,
skims across the roof of the garage,
disappears into dark green undergrowth.
My cat is antsy, pacing.
It's not a day to go out,
which bothers the cat
but suits me just fine.
A breeze drifts through open windows,
and thoughts of other places,
other times
that once stormed through my memory
now shower slowly down with the rain.
My heart is full and grateful—
grateful for the past,
grateful that it's long gone,
grateful that I can gladly let it go.
A lazy rumble of thunder rolls in.
The cat runs,
but this deepest growl of the clouds,
this sharpest bite,
fades to silence
along with those deepest, sharpest memories.

I close my eyes,
lean back and listen
to the chorus of hopeful birdsong
that circles through
the showering rain.

It Came as a Question

It came as a question,
a challenge really—
how would you describe yourself?
(A warning—
don't ask this of an old woman
unless you want to sit for a while,
drift for a while,
sift through life for a while.
Yet there it was,
hanging in the air,
winking from the page—
how would you describe yourself?)
I am like a well-worn shirt,
used to being useful,
washed and worn
again and again,
now soft and comfy and saggy baggy.
I am like a faded flower
that was once bright and lightly scented,
and now perhaps more interesting,
a browning, curling shape.
I am like a warm loaf of freshly baked
homemade bread,
like a pillow fluffed with feathers
where the cat sleeps,
like cream that softens the coffee,
like the dance that has no particular steps,
like the wren singing,
perching, pecking for seeds,
like a blanket around bent shoulders,
like my father's eyes,
like my mother's lips,

like the song that searches for its next line.
How would I describe myself?
I'm the candle in the window at night,
a silent sign to those who've left home
that the light is still on
and the door is always open
for you.

Magical Moon

The moon is magical,
always shifting,
always gifting a glow
not of her making.
She cools the sun's burning blaze,
lets it sift
and drift peacefully
into our night.
But sometimes—
sweet celestial surprise—
she sails into our day.
Look! A child points.
Adults nod. Yes,
an afternoon moon, and—
did you know?—
at the peak of her power, she can
dim that bold sun,
block its light,
darken the day,
cool the earth,
hush birdsong,
shape rare shadows,
and gather the world's watchers
who gasp and whisper
as the trickster makes the sun
disappear,
reminding us all that in the heavens,
she too can take center stage.
But a few hours are enough;
she is soon satisfied
and settles into her old habits,
tide-bringer,

love-teaser,
shape-changer
emptying herself,
filling up again, only to
pour herself out once more.
She is generous,
this elegant,
smiling,
powerful,
magical
moon.

At the Tail End of Winter

Joy is the crocus, who
does not wait for spring
but will push her way up
even through snow
to wake the world.
Fresh and new,
her purple peeks through
undaunted by chill wind,
bright in brown grass,
stretching up as if to say,
"See? Here I am!"
Or rather, "Here we are,"
for she brings sisters with her every year.
They rival the soon-to-come daffodils
and the Lenten roses
to be first to announce
the warm gladness of coming spring
even as the tail end of winter whips by.
Such small blooms,
they can come and go unnoticed.
But for those who watch
for early signs of spring,
the crocus is a generous grace.
She is hope.
She is faithful.
She is bold joy
on a cold day.

A Private Nod

The poet's words, written and flung
into the wildness of my day
became a signpost:
"This is as far as the light
Of my understanding
Has carried me..." she had written*
in an intimate moment of generosity
on the page,
a prompt from someone
I don't even know,
a private nod,
a poetic nudge
to begin exactly there
and follow the trail where
it would take me;
so I wandered that way—
how far has the light
of my understanding
carried me?
To writing in this room with friends,
the sound of traffic
our rushing river,
the rug beneath us
our grassy meadow,
twinkle lights on steel rafters
the heavens above us,
the rustle of writing papers
a breeze sweeping leaves,
our universe a shelter,
our hearts hurt but
healing,
hopeful.

I close my eyes and see us all
in drifts of moonlight
making our way through stars,
out where peace flows,
for we are meditating.
This—yes, this
is as far as my understanding
has carried me,
and for now,
that is far enough.

from "Midlife" by Julie Cadwallader Shaub

From the Hospital Window

I stand at the wide glass window.
Behind me, my son sleeps
in a hospital bed.
My son will be fine—
I am confident of that—
but at the moment,
he is not fine,
so I am not fine either.
I hurt at his pain;
my heart cracks with his cries;
I pray when he hasn't the will
or the faith
to pray.
This present moment,
the Now
is supposed to be a time and place
of meditation and peace.
But this Now, this present moment
bites me.
I look out this wide window
across buildings and treetops.
I see beyond this moment of pain
that curls him inward,
calls all his attention
to a deep
abyss,
and I think even God must cry
at least a little bit every day,
for there's so much to cry about.
I take a deep breath of treetop and sky
and determine to be a source of peace
for my son

just as friends who text me
are a source of peace for me.
This peace connects us
like an invisible, strong thread,
stitching up our cracked hearts
with every color
warm and cool,
joyful and sad,
sometimes glinting with our tears
and God's too.

The Wonder-Work of Winter

We knew it would come—the snow.
It had been forecast for a week.
Still, the child in me cheers
when I wake to the still, soft gray morning
of a snow-covered world.
Every rooftop is a steep hill of white,
sharp edges sculpted smooth.
Snow lines the iron fence railings
and the spiral stairsteps next door.
It outlines tree branches and
rests in plump mounds on flowerpots.
Dollops of snow cream perch on pine branches,
a perfect picture for a holiday card.
Some little creature has left tracks
across the white-carpeted deck—
maybe a 'possum or racoon.
A branch bobs in a thicket of evergreens
and a plop of snow falls.
The branch bobs again;
out pops a sparrow
who proceeds to make his own
wispy tracks across the yard.
I have sisters whose hearts say,
Let's go out! Let's play in the snow,
sled, ski, toss snowballs,
get red-cheeked and cold-nosed
and watch our breath form puffy clouds.
My heart says,
Let's stay inside
wrapped in a warm wool throw.
Let's enjoy this art gallery of windows.
Isn't it a joy to be so different,

some of us snow-babies stepping out,
some of us simply snuggling in,
content to watch the wonder-work,
the artistry of Winter.

A Backyard Chorus Line

A tiny chorus line dressed in green,
the daffodils stood,
posture impeccably straight
as they bordered the backyard garden,
their leaves cupping unopened blooms
waiting in place
to begin their bright show
even as chill winds blew
and snow frosted them white.
A friend suggested that I clip one,
bring it indoors,
put it in water.
It will bloom, she said.
So I slipped one into a vase
in the kitchen window.
Up and out it stretched,
a ruffled center on a star of petals,
a new beginning,
a glad greeting,
a promise of spring.
Then, this week,
the backyard chorus line bloomed,
dancers in yellow,
faces to the sun,
spreading their arms,
nodding their heads,
keeping the promise,
announcing the joy of generous Spring
flinging herself wildly across the land,
bringing life out of dead-looking Winter.
She cheers us on with her extravagance,
her rich kaleidoscope of hope-filled messages.

The squares on the calendar say
that Spring is a few weeks away,
but already I hear her song.
Even now I see her smile.

The Sun Yawned

It's the first day of Spring.
With a slow stretch,
the sun yawns into the deep, still sea of sky,
softens the clear, cloudless blue,
reddens the top branches of the elms,
slowly slides its smiling light down the trunks.
I watch from my upstairs window.
Oh, Spring, at times
I thought you had forgotten us.
But your name is on the calendar square.
I've underlined it.
And here you are!
Warmth is drifting through the air, I think,
anticipating a day without a coat,
maybe even without a sweater.
I'm thinking bluebirds,
white blossoms on the dogwood,
seeds to be planted,
spring-fresh air to breathe.
Then I notice the roof of the first floor
just beneath my window.
The shingles glitter with frost.
I flick my phone to the weather.
Twenty-six degrees.
Twenty-six!
Oh, Winter,
you may be gone,
but in your wake, you've left a chill.
Of course you have,
for it's only
the first day of Spring.

Caught by Surprise

On the way to the kitchen,
two steps past the dining room window,
I pause.
I had barely glanced outside in passing,
having already witnessed the scene of early spring—
hackberries still bare-branched from winter,
the dogwood's gray limbs holding up leaf buds
like tiny green candle flames,
the rust colored, dried blooms of a rhododendron
that flowered too early and froze back into fall colors.
It was a flash of pink that caught me by surprise.
Pink?
I step back to the window
for a second look.
A newly planted azalea peers back at me,
low and close to the mulched garden
in my neighbor's yard.
And very pink.
I wasn't expecting pink.
Winter was so raw,
so kill-the-plants frigid
that I've been intent on discovering what survived.
Bit by bit, life was revealing itself—
Lenten roses in holy white,
daffodils and forsythia in sun-kissed yellow,
violets gowned in deep, regal purple,
Nature's parade of spring fashion.
Yes, these I knew.
These, I had seen.
But now this fancy, frilly pink azalea
waves in the wind and fairly shouts,
"Look at me!"

And, of course, I do,
marveling at the appearance of this cheeky pink plant
flaunting herself,
loud and bright,
proud in my neighbor's garden,
and worth a second look.
So of course, I do,
and I will,
again and again
until the whole neighborhood
is alive with spring.

I Imagined Fog Drifting In

Steep narrow stairs spiraled up
past a small kitchen and parlor,
past even smaller bedrooms
on the upper floors.
At the top of the lighthouse,
I stepped out onto a walkway
circling the towering lens.
Fresh breeze,
choppy waves,
a clear sky all the way
from hazardous coast to horizon.
I imagined fog drifting in,
wild waves crashing,
night falling.
I imagined sailors
squinting through a foggy night,
cresting a wave,
sliding into a trough,
land somewhere near–
but where?
Then a glint of light.
It comes again.
Here I am,
the lighthouse signals,
through the fog,
in the night,
I am standing,
I am shining,
I am here,
and you will find your way.
If you are sailing rough seas,
watch for lighthouses.

They are there.
If you are on solid ground,
keep standing,
keep shining,
take care of your flame,
for someone is squinting,
watching and waiting
for glimmers of hope
in the fog.

Roof Ornament

The robin sits on the apex
of the garage next door
as if he is the sentinel,
the lookout,
for bird world.
He looks left and right,
bobs his head,
preens his flight feathers,
scans the backyard scene again.
He's a living roof ornament,
his plump rust-orange belly topping off
the brown-shingled A-line roof
and tan stucco walls
as if some designer had chosen him—
exactly him—
and carefully placed him there.
And perhaps some Designer did.

Except for the Violets

"Everything is terrible," she said,
"except for daffodils."
I nodded.
Everything seems so, so terrible—
except the daffodils are blooming.
And the lenten roses.
And forsythia and saucer magnolias.
Cherry blossoms tumble in the breeze
like spring snow.
Everything is terrible—
except for the violets scattered across the lawn
and the purple-red blossoms on the redbuds.
The hyacinths' perfume smells heavenly.
Newborn leaves, feather-fine
sprout on the tulip poplar.
The whole treescape wears a green sheen.
Bluebirds are moving into the birdhouse.
Doves, cardinals, chickadees, sparrows
sing welcome to the warmth of spring.
Children run and play, smile and laugh.
I hold out both of my hands, palms up.
In one, I feel the weight of everything terrible,
in the other, the fullness of everything good,
for goodness and beauty have weight too.
I try to find the balance.
I wish all people,
everyone everywhere,
could hold only goodness, kindness, beauty.
But life has never been that way.
Maybe someday?
For now, I close my hand around the terrible,
feel it as a hard, jagged rock.

I cannot let it go, for it is real and demanding,
and I cry for it,
for I know that it does not have to be.
But then there is my other hand,
my always open hand,
holding the weight of goodness,
which is surprisingly firm and powerful
even as it sits soft as a butterfly on my palm.
Goodness, kindness, beauty—
in this hand is life,
creating and recreating,
loving and laughing,
always growing like spring.
This open hand is for sharing,
especially when it seems that everything is terrible.
Yes, there is this hard, jagged, hurtful rock,
but look—
see?
There is also a butterfly.

Painted with Joy

Last night's drenching rain has left
the morning air cooler,
peacefully breezy,
the sky flecked with drifts of cloud,
the earth dripping color—
brilliant yellows,
rich greens,
deep reds,
velvety blues—
a fresh day of spacious,
gracious spring
painted with the joy of re-creation.
A gray cat tiptoes
through regal irises,
around dogwood dressed in wedding white,
between coral azaleas
in a raindrop-sparkled garden.
The world is full of wonder
at its newborn self.

Not the Off-Hand "Thanks"

"Nature calms me," said my grandson
as he stepped into his backyard,
left the stress of the school day,
entered the grace of afternoon.
I wish I had been that wise
when I was seven.
But nature is a patient teacher and
waited years for me to pause
at the call of a cardinal,
linger over the unfolding coneflower,
inhale the scent of honeysuckle,
finger the curling bark of the crape myrtle,
taste the wild strawberry,
settle my soul.
Nature waited years for me to be
deeply grateful,
and for me,
that's where true peace begins.
I can't imagine peace without gratitude—
not the off-hand, easily tossed "thanks"
but the gratitude that has no words,
the awe of a heart
full of the richness of being.
There is, of course, a dark side,
the underside of living,
but that's all the more reason
to follow the wisdom of a seven-year-old
and at least once in a while
step into the grace
of Nature.

Growing Up With the Wind

I grew up with the wind
always whipping the scrub brush,
whistling at the windows,
whooshing in gusts at the open door,
hot and dusty and dry in the summer,
blowing dust storms to town,
making the sky brown,
picking up tumbleweeds
and rolling them down the street
like straw bowling balls,
sometimes swirling and speeding up
to tornado strength—
and in the winter,
barreling in straight from the north,
icy and nipping,
cold steel in its breath,
pushing me back as I tried to walk forward.
There was no hope for a hairstyle—
we wore the windblown look—
unless we plastered our hair with Aquanet,
and then how strange!
Everything blowing, bending, flapping
except hair, frozen in place, defiant
and totally unnatural.
Then at some point,
winter drifted into spring,
and though the wind blew as hard as ever,
it brought the comforting,
happy, hopeful scent of rain.
When the rain finally came,
it fell sideways in sheets,
in thrall to the wind.

Wind was a constant fierce presence
that flowed as it pleased
over, around, or through
fences, houses,
scrawny trees,
which bent and bowed to its will.
The airport windsock was never limp.
The flag at school flapped constantly,
its tethering rope sharply slapping the pole
in a metallic rhythm—
ping, ping, ping.
Walking meant holding onto skirts, scarves,
sweaters, coats, hats.
The wind wanted to whip them up and away.
In play?
Sometimes it felt playful.
Other times it was annoying.
Sometimes it was downright scary.
But it has always been a friend,
the wind.

At the Edge of My Coffee

A tiny bubble
at the edge of my coffee
reflects my kitchen windows
in miniature,
a visual echo of daylight drifting in
on a cool, rainy day,
a calm take-your-time afternoon.
Peace comes in the wink of a bubble
at the edge
of my coffee
at the edge
of my thoughts
at the edge
of my hopes for the day.

Looking Up

I really should remember
to look up more often.
True, there are wonders to see
by looking down,
small delights that surprise,
but it's up that fills my soul
with hope,
with promise,
with possibility.
Up to that place
where the tip-tops of elms and oaks
brush the sky.
Where trees stretch and reach and grow,
my heart also stretches and reaches and grows.
Where trees dance in the breeze,
my heart also dances.
Trees are silent, steady, strong,
their limbs like arms open wide
in total trust.
Abandon worry, they seem to say.
No reliving the past,
no preliving the future.
Inhabit the deep breath of Now.
This quiet counsel comes
from their wise old selves.
I should remind my wise old self
to look up more often,
to pause and breathe
and heed the counsel of trees.

I Saw You

I saw you from the back porch
where I sat in my rocking chair,
you on the beach beside the lake,
taking your time,
lining up toys.
The toy line was long
and you were strong
for such a little boy,
tan, footprints dimpling the sand.
A dump truck went here, just so,
a sandy horseshoe,
a shovel and pail upside down,
and who knows where the line goes.
I suspect even you don't know,
running here and there,
placing and gracing the beach
with each toy,
each rock,
each block of wood
tossed aside by the teenager who cuts the lawn.
The wood is of no use to him,
but to you it's a treasure.
Watching you from the back porch,
that is my treasure.

And Still They Come

In dark silhouette,
a flock of birds
darts,
swift and low,
across a sky cloaked in clouds of gray
in shades that drift
and slowly shift,
now light,
now dark.
Wind, heavy with weather, quickens.
Air thickens.
Branches wag their fingers at the sky.
And still they come,
scores of birds,
arrows speeding,
reading the signs of the clouds,
believing the whine of the wind.
They look so sure of where they're going.
Some inborn knowing of nature
sends them racing past the trees,
against the breeze.
Are they seeking shelter?
Outrunning the rain?
Or simply celebrating
wings and wind
and the miracle of uplift
on a fresh tide of air
as rain begins to fall.

Butterfly

The butterfly was so small
with yellow wings—
a sulfur, I think it's called.
It looked so happy flitting
among the petunias,
a bright spot gliding and dipping
into the pink and purple.
The cat watched, fascinated,
and unable to simply watch, of course,
being a cat,
swatted at the butterfly,
brought it down.
It fluttered,
tried to rise
but was no match for the cat's paw
and jaw,
for the cat lapped it up,
that fluttery, buttery yellow-winged thing,
and swallowed it down
in one gulp.
After all,
the butterfly was so small.

The Deep Knowing of a Stone

It fits perfectly in my palm,
this rock I found,
heavy, flat, and smooth,
from a riverbed maybe.
It's a warm, gray-brown,
the color of a rabbit
hiding in plain sight
and just as still.
It would be easy to stack
with other stones,
to create a calming cairn
or to line a labyrinth to linger in.
But maybe it's meant to simply be held,
a touchstone.
Its curves and weight hold comfort,
solid, sure, simple,
worn and weathered,
dimpled and scratched.
I turn it over and over in my hand
as if I might find a message on it.
There are no engraved words,
but it does hold a message.
I cradle this stone in both hands,
for it holds a deep knowing:
Let the river rage on, it says.
Let it smooth out your rough edges.
Find purpose in stillness.
Be a calming, settled soul.
Outlast the flood.

Slipped Between the Pages

I grabbed the nearest piece of paper,
slipped it between pages-read and not-read in
wife/daughter/self by Beth Kephart, a favorite writer.
I shoved the book into my carry-on
and dashed out to catch a flight to Texas
to visit my dad, rich in years at 95 and,
to his consternation, confined to a wheelchair.
By the time I arrived, he was,
to his consternation, confined to his bed
and being fed
by caregivers.
A day went by,
two,
three,
until the morning he couldn't eat
and hardly roused from sleep.
"Have you ever heard a death rattle?"
a caregiver asked.
I had not—
until that day,
that day he raised his arms,
reached for the sky,
opened his eyes,
gazed beyond the ceiling,
and then left us
for something more.
Days later, standby on a flight home,
I took the last seat on the plane
and slipped my paper boarding pass
between the same pages of the same book.
I had not read any farther,
did not read on the flight,

but found comfort holding *wife/daughter/self*.
A week later, by the light of early evening,
I settled in to read,
my place marked by two slips of paper.
The first was a card from a bouquet
from one of my sons:
"Happy Mother's Day! We love you."
The other was the boarding pass
that meant leaving my father
for the last time.
As the light dimmed, there I sat,
holding two cards, one book, and me.
I had slipped between the pages of life,
somewhere between parents and children,
closing one chapter,
turning the page to another,
and hoping for a happy ending.

If I Take the Hint

As I stepped outside,
a swirl of white petals—cherry blossoms—
floated down like snowflakes,
settled silently at my feet.
My yard has no cherry trees,
but a neighbor's yard does,
and the wind has lifted them,
drifted them,
gifted them to me,
celebrating the world reborn.
So many of Spring's gifts are small—
a yard carpeted in violets,
forsythia gone wild with yellow blooms,
shadows of breeze-blown trees
rippling like creek water in dawn's lemony light.
But truly, I see the world reborn
any time I pause,
from reliving
or preliving
and begin, instead, just living,
noticing the moment—
for a moment—
which is all I can manage
most of the time.
But Nature has a way of nudging me into
the Now—
white petals flutter past,
shadows ripple in lemon light,
long-limbed forsythia waves in the wind.
If I take the hint,
I am also reborn,
and each step I take
can be
the first.

The Thinnest of Tightropes

Good morning, tiny spider.
I see that overnight,
you've made the thinnest of tightropes
beside my kitchen sink
between the soap dispenser
and the window ledge.
There you perch,
right in the center.
I actually thought you were
a tiny ant caught in spider silk
until I looked closer.
You are not safe here.
I gently lift you
on a small piece of cardboard
from the recycle bin.
I hope you don't run up my arm,
because as small as you are,
I'm afraid I would instinctively,
and quickly,
brush you off,
and that might be a traumatic event
for you.
So as I head for the back door,
I'm glad to see that you stay put—
for a second.
Then you skitter to the edge of the cardboard
and bungee jump off,
spinning your own lifeline as you dive.
At first I think you've gone to the floor,
but, no, there you are,
dangling from your silken thread.
You ride there,

swaying gently as I open the door
and step outside.
I place you, string first,
at the edge of an empty bucket,
trusting that through your day of
adventures,
you'll find a safe place to settle.
Godspeed, tiny spider.
If you should ever come back
to visit my kitchen,
you would be welcome—
at least for a minute.

The Song of All-is-Done

A steady swish and swash
whispers from the dishwasher.
The tide of soap and water
swiftly ebbs and flows
like splashing waves,
white noise,
the song of all-is-done,
all-is-well,
no more urgency of
clattering silverware,
clinking dishes,
stirring peppers and potatoes,
cracking eggs,
buttering,
salting,
tasting,
serving,
clearing.
All is done for the day.
I sit by lamplight,
cat in my lap,
book open to the next chapter
to read,
to rest,
to doze to the song
of the sea in a box
and imagine that I'm at the ocean,
waves shushing me,
wind feathering my hair,
my toes in the sand,
leaving footprints as I stroll
along the shore.

This evening,
listening to the swashing song
of day-is-done,
I stroll the shore of my thoughts.
Perhaps even there,
I will leave footprints.

What the Bee Sees

Lean close to summer blooms,
peek into petunias,
dive deep into daylilies,
stare boldly at black-eyed Susans,
push past flashy petals
into the center,
the inner sanctum,
anthers and stamen,
tiny flying flags
or miniature stars
or prickly pillows
dusty with pollen,
maybe moist with the season's
sweet dew.
This is what the bee must see
as he follows the path
of a petal's dark veins
to settle headfirst,
to nestle inside
for a moment
or two.
The butterfly flicks
her curling, unfurling,
thread-thin tongue
to taste this splendor.
The ant tiptoes in,
humble on this holy ground,
this extravagant gift.
It's our gift too
for the mere price
of a moment's noticing.
Peek in.

Dive deep.
Lean close.
Stare boldly.
See what the bee sees.

What if You Were the Wind?

What if you were the wind
flowing 'round the world
in a whirl of hot and cold,
bold enough to blow a house down,
then a day later,
shy of the sky,
whispery, shushing, hiding,
slyly slipping around trees.
What if you roared through mountain passes,
lapped at ocean waves,
played havoc with sand,
then ran out of gusts
to sigh and sway,
breezy, sneezy,
tousling the grain in the field.
What if you nosed through a bubble wand,
puffed out a cheeky bubble.
What if you tossed the bubble,
twirled and swirled it
until it danced into a yard down the street.
What if you were that iridescent bubble,
flickering soapy red and green and yellow
as you rolled on the breeze
and laughed at the neighbor who looked up
just as you floated by
dipping, bobbing, and
pop!
What if you were the neighbor
who looked up just in time
to see the bubble pop,
and you stopped
to smile awhile.

Oh, but you are the wind,
the bubble,
the neighbor.
At least you were
for these past few minutes.

I Know Nothing

I know nothing except that
the cat jumps into my lap every evening
and settles in,
purring as if all is right
in her cat-centric world.

I know nothing except
the feel of the pillow beneath my head,
cushioning me,
holding me
for hours on end.

I know nothing except that
the mockingbird has somehow decided
that my yard is his,
and the rabbit that lives out back
has claimed what the bird has left open.

I know nothing except that
the flavor of dark chocolate
still satisfies me in a way
that milk chocolate doesn't.

I know nothing except that
my own heart on this day
is full of roller-coaster feelings,
zig-zag and see-saw
crest the hill,
careen down the other side,
and I know nothing except the fact
that I will hold on
and ride it as long as I possibly can.

I know nothing except that
I am here.
I am breathing.
I am feeling.
Deeply feeling.
I am here,
healing and whole.

So Many Reasons

The sky is crying today,
softly, slowly dripping tears down my windows.
And why wouldn't it?
The world is rumbling, tumbling,
churning, turning,
so much hurt,
so much hate,
so many reasons to cry.
But past the teardrops on my window screen,
I can see two squirrels
skittering up the trunk of a pine tree,
its branches stretching high
brushing away the tears in the crying sky.
The two squirrels have made a runway
through the deep green maze of pines.
They scamper in stops and starts up and down.
On the way up, they carry bundles of fresh
spring leaves they've nibbled off the bushes below.
They're building a nest near the tip-top
in a thicket of pine needles.
It's almost invisible, a dark bulk
nestled between branches,
swaying in the breeze.
I assume squirrels do this every spring—
build their penthouse nests—
but this is the first time I've seen them
carrying greenery,
refurbishing their nursery.
I suppose they know what they're doing,
trusting swaying pines
not to toss them out but to rock them,
not to crash but cradle them.

So I'm trusting those little squirrels
and the pine trees too.
I'm trusting the return of spring,
the bloom of dogwood,
the robin hopping along the porch rail.
Trees sway,
skies cry,
the world churns,
but we will gather fresh bundles of hope,
carry them along the mazes of our world,
jump the chasms,
bridge the gaps,
and build at the very top,
stretching high into the crying sky
to brush away the tears.

One of These Days

So . . . I'm not going to cook anymore.
No heating oil in the pan,
or chopping ingredients for stir-fry.
No more washing the veggies
and peeling and paring and dicing.
No more mixing and kneading
dough for bread.
No more timing chicken
and roasted vegetables in the oven.
No more toasting pine nuts
and dicing tomatoes
and stuffing acorn squash.
Just making room
for the rest of my life here.
Rest as in the remaining future from here on out.
Also rest as in feet-up, comfy chair,
good book, doze-worthy moments.
I've done my time,
prepared the meals,
catered to tastes other than mine,
packed the snacks,
washed the dishes—
oh yes, that's included, the dishes.
No more cooking,
no more washing.
One of these days,
one of these days,
one of these days
I'm not going to cook anymore.

Afraid I Might Fall

Sometimes there are no words,
there's only sitting in silence
and letting the tears come.
It feels massively important to lose
a father.
I'm left with roots running deep,
but the trellis is gone,
the one that held me up,
the one too often taken for granted.
There is now a breeze at my back
where the support used to be,
and I'm afraid I might fall,
but I am finding I'm strong enough
to stand
on my own,
and I realize that all these years
I have been strong.
And all these years,
he knew.

Bluebird Between Storms

Between storms,
the whipping wind calms
to an easy breeze
flicking rainwater off
the newborn leaves.
Mama bluebird flits to her birdhouse
with thin dried stems of grass
dangling
from her beak.
She pauses at the entrance,
the just-right-size hole,
glances around,
spies a robin at the birdbath.
Satisfied that he is busy drinking,
she ducks into her house,
reappears seconds later, empty-beaked,
and darts away.
Papa bluebird watches
at a distance
atop a light post
as the robin decides to perch
on the roof of the bluebirds' house.
Mama bluebird flies back with more straw
but stops short,
resting on a garden ornament,
a shepherds' crook,
wary of the robin,
this unwelcome visitor.
Papa bluebird casually glides closer
then dives at the robin,
who decides it's best to be gone.
Mama bluebird flits in again and,

with a wink of blue from her tail,
disappears into her house.
Bluebird wisdom says
be patient
when someone needs to rest
atop your house,
but keep the boundaries clear,
for it is, indeed, your house,
and it is you who are building
your nesting place there.
It's what we do
in the pause
between storms.

Ah, the Dahlia

In the warming days of spring,
I planted two spidery tubers,
dahlias-to-be.
They soon sent up shoots,
greening, growing,
straight stems,
branching arms,
arrowed, light-veined leaves.
I watched for blooms to form,
for I had forgotten what color
they would be,
and I love the surprise of dahlias.
One bloomed in midsummer,
petals the color of burgundy wine.
The other grew taller,
stretched her leaves,
but gave no sign of blooms.
I made excuses for her.
(I am an expert at excuses,
being a late bloomer myself.)
Maybe it's the heat, I said.
It's been awfully hot this summer.
Maybe it's because she came from
the supermarket, not the nursery.
Maybe I gave her too much water.
Or not enough.
I never know.
The fire-red salvia came and went,
the peppery basil is going to seed,
even the fragrant mint has bloomed.
I began to think this dahlia
would be content to wear green

all her life.
(Late bloomer that I am,
I've not outgrown impatience.)
Then this week,
two blooms uncurled,
unfurled,
creamy peach,
warm blushing joy.
I had forgotten what her name was,
if the package even said.
Some dahlias are named Beauty
or Charlotte
or White Moonlight.
I call this one
Patience,
for that is the wisdom she carries:
Plant beauty, kindness, grace,
she says,
then be at peace;
be
patient.

The Bell Tower

A rainy day,
silver showers,
drips tapping gently on windowpanes,
soft sounds soothe until
chimes ring out the hour
on the campus to the east.
Those chimes.
What a nuisance they were twenty years ago
when the bell tower was built,
ringing every quarter hour—really?
Apparently, measuring time
in fifteen minute intervals
is important. To someone.
I prefer a less metered flow of hours.
Then, sometime in those twenty years,
it happened:
The chimes marking time
faded into the soundtrack of my day.
Now when I notice them,
I wonder—what else has faded?
In the unbounded, wide-ranging time of my mind,
what else ebbs into the background?
The chimes bring me back to the present moment,
to the chorus of birdsong,
the tick of an old clock,
the tink of ice in a glass,
the chip of a chipmunk,
the buzz of insects tucked in the shadows of bushes,
the breeze whispering, "Come back.
Come back to this place.
Come back to this time.
Come back to the chimes."

They're ringing again now.
Through silver showers,
a quarter hour
has come
and gone.

A Game of War I Don't Want to Play

He's being cranky again, my young grandson,
corralling me into a game of war
I do not want to play,
the swingset the villain's lair.
I don't like war, I tell him.
I don't like fighting.
I like peace.
He says, "First you fight the monsters,
and then you go to your place of peace."
I look up,
up to the treetops,
take a deep breath.
I don't tell him that I have some experience
in fighting monsters who were not quite
as imaginary as his.
Or were they?
I also don't tell him
that I don't always win.
The treetops sway,
the breeze whispers peace.
I look back at my grandson.
"Okay," I say.
"I will fight your monsters."
And my heart breaks a little,
because I know that I will.

The Moon was Half

The moon was half tonight,
a white porcelain bowl perched
on a thin shelf of hackberry branches
brushing the night sky.
I wanted to reach out,
to cup it in my palms like
a bowl of soup
or an extra large cocoa.
I wanted to drink from it
a magical sweet moonlight.
Surely it would be smooth,
deliciously moon flavored,
a taste that only those who've sipped
the milk of the moon would know.
It would satisfy and warm with wonder,
make the eyes sparkle,
make the smile serene.
A child would notice and ask,
"Why are you so happy?"
and I would answer, "Ah,
it's because the moon
was half tonight,
and I am full to overflowing."

A Gardener's Optical Illusion

A trick of morning light,
a slant of glass in a windowpane,
and I see a bevy of black-eyed Susans
where there are none.
The real golden, black-eyed blooms
bob on long stems to the south of my back door.
Their reflection sprawls across
the window-framed view to the west,
which happens to be the neighbor's garage
and has never sprouted flowers.
Yet there it is
from my vantage point indoors,
an optical illusion,
a mirage,
a golden, pop-up garden,
a gift of sun and glass.
I wonder if a good memory is like that,
a reality, once tangible,
reflecting now from a window of the soul
so that for a moment,
the mind's eye sees a golden scene,
hears it,
smells it,
tastes it,
feels it
and knows it as a gift,
knows that this reflection is
no trick,
no mirage,
but is imprinted forever
on the pane of the heart.

The Thread Connecting Us

The silver SUV pulled out of the driveway
as my son and his young family headed
to the airport
after the holidays.
I don't suppose they saw me
wave them out of sight.
I don't suppose they knew my throat was thick,
my shoulders heavy,
my eyes blinking fast to block the tears.
I hadn't meant to cry,
but my mind pulled up a years-ago memory
of a hot blue-sky Texas morning
when it was my young family
pulling away from Mom and Dad's house,
and I looked back to see my dad
standing on the front porch
waving us out of sight.
At that moment, I instinctively knew why—
why he watched,
why he waved,
why he waited
until he could no longer see us—
maybe longer, who knows?
He was holding the thread of connection
as long as he could,
knowing it might be the last time he saw us.
It wasn't—
not then.
He could not know,
nor could I,
that my sisters and I would be with him
for the last goodbye,

and that in my memory,
he is still on that front porch,
waving as the distance grows between us,
just as I wave to my children and grandchildren,
holding the thread of connection
as long as I can,
for they always leave
with a good part
of my heart.

A Gift of Poppies

A friend shared her garden with me
in a baggie of poppy seeds,
tiny black things
that could be mistaken
for a swarm of gnats.
I had my doubts that they would grow,
for I am a haphazard gardener.
But I do love the look of delicate,
showy, confident poppies,
so I planted the seeds.
Those tiny black dots sprouted and stretched
into tall, slender stalks
that birthed frilly-edged blooms of
rosy pink with inner brush-strokes of lavender
around a globe-shaped center,
a tiny pumpkin-like pod of yellow and green.
I wish poppies would bloom all summer,
but petals faded,
fluttered,
fell from their centers,
those small, round globes,
each now regally topped with a tiny crown.
Then something astonishing happened.
As the globes browned,
under their crowns,
tiny holes appeared
like observation windows for gnats—
or, as it happens,
escape hatches for seeds.
Stems dry, weaken,
bend in the wind.
Out fall the seeds and scatter on the ground.

My grandson said, "Pretty soon poppies
will cover your whole yard,
because you get more and more each season."
And I nod,
for that is how gracious a garden is,
how generous.
One plant multiplies its beautiful, bountiful self
in tiny seed-promises,
packets of hope for the year to come.
And if I pluck the seed pods
before they spill,
I can shake seeds out of their windows
and into a baggie
to share with a friend
these tiny black things
that could be mistaken
for a swarm of gnats
but are really a gift of beauty
and bounty
and hope
and grace.

No Hurry, No Worry

The elms are late-bloomers.
Maples, redbuds, tulip poplars,
even grandfather hackberry
show off their spring green leaves.
But the elms,
one in each corner of my back yard,
are still asleep.
My young neighbor says,
"I think they are dead."
I squint and study the elms,
look them up and down
as if he might be right,
but I know he's not.
Silhouetted against the morning sky,
their upreaching branches hold bumps of
leaves-to-be
and the faint sheen of
newborn green.
My elms bide their time.
No hurry.
No worry.
I imagine that's their mantra,
their peaceful way of entering spring,
stretching and yawning,
catching a few more drowsy minutes.
These elms have seen seasons come and go
for at least as long as I have,
and they know the deep joy of
lingering
a moment
longer.
They know the deep peace of

unhurried progress,
the contentment of
being a
late bloomer.

Where Does the Music Go?
for Jeanette and Doug

After the last notes are sung
and the last chord drifts into silence,
where does the music go?
Maybe it mingles with a pulsing energy
of all the notes ever sung,
all the rhythms ever played,
surrounding us in a symphony of sound
beyond what we can hear,
swelling and fading and swelling
again and again,
coloring the universe
with our sorrows and joys,
our fears and our hopes.

After the last notes of our Sunday songs,
after the last chords rise into the air,
where does the music go?
It settles into our spirits,
sings in our hearts,
hums in the deep of the night
when sleep won't come.
It calms fears,
soothes the breaking heart,
underscores our days.
Music is the lullaby that births us,
the comfort that accompanies our death.

Ours is the gift to make music,
to hear music,
to hear into the music,
to hear through the music,

to hear beyond the music
the heartbeat of heaven,
the hum of God.

This is what you do for us.
This is what you give us.
Thank you.

Peace, They Insist

A trio of peace lilies stands tall
at my back window.
Raindrop-shaped upper leaves
curve over pebbled flower stalks
like hands gently cupping a candle
to protect it from a draft.
I imagine these upper leaves
shielding these symbols of peace
from today's blast of bad news,
war and destruction,
hunger and hurt,
clenched fists, bared teeth,
faces distorted with anger.
How can these flowers stand quietly
proclaiming peace, peace, peace
in such a time of tension?
And yet they do, and they have.
Year after year,
decade after decade,
in calm, in turbulence,
peace lilies have stood tall in our world.
Today's sunlight drifts in,
glows through dark lower leaves
and light upper leaves
translucent as stained-glass windows.
Peace, the lilies insist,
sharing their ancient wisdom,
and I see that peace is many-layered.
I cannot wave a wand and win world peace.
I cannot change minds and hearts
of those who hold tight to hatred.
I cannot control the uncontrollable.

But the inner layer of peace
is heart deep.
I can cup my own flame,
maybe yours too.
Maybe we can shield each other
from the cutting wind.
Maybe we can be translucent,
let the light glow through us.
Maybe we can stand tall for peace.
It's said that often,
in the wild,
peace lilies grow in colonies.
I will stand alone if I have to,
but I believe we are a colony.
I am looking beyond my back window.
I'm aiming to grow
and glow
peace
in the wild.

What the Chipmunk Told Me

"Hello, chipmunk," I said.

The chipmunk blinked,
her cheeks full.
Then she nodded.
"Mmmph."
And scampered away.

I sat back,
watched her go.
I think she lives
near the neighbor's drainpipe,
where water whooshes down
from the gutters
in a torrent
when it rains.
I wondered about her then—
is she ever in danger of
being flooded out?

While I was wondering this,
she appeared again,
cocked her head and said,
"I thought you'd never notice."

"Notice?" I asked.
"I notice you every day
pouching leftover birdseed."

"I thought you would never
notice enough
to address me."

She smiled—
I swear she smiled—
"And now that you have,"
she cleared her throat,
"I will tell you
what I think."

"What?
I leaned closer.

"I think you should worry less
and notice
more."

The Magic of the Ordinary

I would say it's magical—
although it can be explained—
the way the pepper bush hides
within a pale, flat, round seed
snuggled in the warm dirt,
the way it wakes only when it's ready,
the way it unfurls arrow-shaped leaves,
stretches thin arms to bask in sunshine,
flirts with wind,
revels in rain,
and smiles in small white blooms.
I know this can be explained,
but it seems magical,
the way those blooms shed petals
and take on pale green skin,
the way they curve and grow longer each day,
turning gold,
blushing orange,
deepening to red,
every day ripening
smooth, shiny, plump.
I pluck them free,
split them,
scoop out scores of seeds,
pale, flat, round,
magic,
for inside each
hides a pepper bush ready to emerge
when the time is right.
I dice these plump, ripe peppers,
stir-fry them,
taste their snappy sweetness,

and marvel at the goodness of the garden.
All of this can be explained,
I know.
But I say
it's magical.

The Word that Waved

Has a word ever waved to you
from something you were reading,
like a kid in school, hand held high,
Me! Me! Choose me!
The word "expansive" waved to me,
sat up and saluted,
highlighted itself.
I paused,
right then,
right there,
hooked and held.
Expansive.
The word unfolds
like opening hands,
arms swinging out,
stretching,
reaching beyond.
Expansive
raises my head,
puts a smile on my face
fills me with a feeling of all's well.
Expansive says,
"Here is the gift,
sun warming your face,
breath of air flicking your hair,
call-and-response, bird to bird,
scent of blooming and greening things,
the embrace of invisible strands
of love and goodness
weaving through the universe,
vining and twining and blooming
in small acts of generous grace

or large acts of courage and kindness.
Expansive says
there is room—
room for you,
room for me,
room for all of us
in this universe of abundant,
all-embracing
love and goodness
that flow freely
like light seeping through cracks,
like springwater bubbling up through rocks,
like breezes drifting through open windows.
Love and goodness
find their way,
refuse to be bound,
refuse to be hoarded,
grow and overflow.
They wave—"Choose me"—
for love and goodness
are forever and always
expansive.

Perching on my Roof

I have a mockingbird—
for how long, I don't know;
he is free to come and go
but, for now, perches on my roof
outside my window
running through his repertoire
in all the bird-languages,
as if he has decided one song
is not enough to express
his ecstatic heart,
so he weaves tunes end to end,
high and low,
lilting and liquid,
warbled and chirped,
a celebration of sound
dancing through my open window,
waking me to this one day.
Tomorrow, he may be on another roof,
regaling no one in particular,
for he needs no audience,
he would sing at the top of his little lungs
even if no one was listening.
But today, I am listening,
pausing in the early stillness
to hear this songster
dressed in stately gray,
serenading my morning
with flowing melodies
flung freely into the breeze.
Whatever the day may bring,
my mockingbird has already
sung the sweetness into my world.

I Spy

I spy something green
and it starts with a T,
and you know (knowing me)
that it's a tree,
a carefree tree,
for the carefree me
of childhood.
Grown-ups are never really care free,
because there's too much to care about.
I now spy anger,
grief,
hurt.
Sometimes I want to close my eyes
and spy
nothing at all.
Sometimes it seems as if the whole world
has gone mad
and squeezed the life out of life.
But even behind closed eyes,
I spy something green,
something growing,
and I return
to the childhood game—
but with one change:
I spy…something beautiful.
For there is always beauty
of some kind, somewhere.
And goodness and love.
I care about these, too.
Even now, I spy beauty
in a summer-full tree,
a billow of leaves

bowing in the breeze,
waving to three geese winging across
an evening sky the color of wishes
and strawberry ice cream.
A firefly winks in the cool dark of a hedge.
I catch the scent of newly bloomed jasmine.
I spy beauty.
And goodness.
And kindness.
That's a game I need
no matter where I am,
no matter what else I spy.
It's a game I must play
with my whole heart,
because it keeps me hopeful,
because in the end,
it's not a game.

Silent Green Tongues and Blushing Petals

The sun peeked out once today.
Clouds barely gave way,
then slipped back across her bright face.
"Our day," they said.
And, truly, it was.
They cried,
softly, quietly,
leaving tears in droplets
on window screens,
on the silent green tongues of lily leaves,
on the blushing petals of Lenten roses.
The wind sighed.
"It will pass," she said.
And, truly, it did,
for the clouds moved on
to weep somewhere else,
and the sun smiled.

One Glance

One glance out the window was enough
to nudge me
to set aside the tomato I'd been washing.
After a muted day of low-bellied,
slow-drizzle clouds,
the setting sun had broken through
with a gold-green light
that drew me to step outside
into strands of straight-down sun-silvered rain.
And there it was,
as I'd sensed it would be,
arcing big and bright in the east,
bridging north and south on the horizon,
shimmering blue and indigo
vibrant violet,
brilliant green,
decadent red and orange,
bold yellow
in a bow framing the curve of the world
with an embrace of all that is,
a benediction for life
in all its glorious color and variety,
reveling in all the different ways of being,
all kinds of beauty,
all the paths to hope and joy and love
and peace,
sunset beaming through rain
with a parting, glorious gift
that could so easily have gone unseen,
but discovered in a chance glance
out the window.
One glance was enough

to set aside the tomato.
One glance was enough
to discover the prism'd gift
of a sunset in the rain.

With a Flash of Wings

You're a topsy-turvy,
upside-down eater,
a sleek seeker of seeds,
my little nuthatch friend.
You cling tail up
to the green metal mesh
and poke around
for a sunflower seed,
but you find none
because I failed to fill the feeder.
By the time I bring my bag of seeds,
you have flown.
I unhook your empty pantry and
pour in a waterfall of seeds.
Rushing,
tumbling
sunflower grains,
shiny dark
speckled with white,
they pile up,
a feast for the feathered.
Before I can rehang the feeder,
you dash in
with a flash of wings,
and I freeze.
The feeder dangles from my fingers.
For a moment, you perch,
topsy-turvy, upside-down,
then snatch a snack
and dart away,
wings waving.
Sleek little beak-down clown,

you are brave to come so close.
Did you think I was a flower?
I'm wearing blossom pink—
not my favorite color,
but maybe yours?
Whatever you thought,
your presence was a compliment.
You made my heart glad,
and I thank you.

The Gift of Permission

Beyond the big occasions,
the wide open doors,
the graduation,
the successful job interview,
the births and birthdays,
it's the small things that have given me
the greatest permission.
The gift of a dark-haired, dark-eyed
baby doll
after dozens of blonde, blue-eyed dolls,
giving me permission to change.
The bouquet of pink rosebuds
to ten-year-old me,
giving me permission to grow up.
A thin book of collected poems
giving me permission to seek wisdom
among poets.
Music in a dim room
with no one watching,
giving me permission to dance.
A slip of paper, my name on it,
in a chair in the choir loft
giving me permission to belong.
A tray of paints
and a blank piece of paper,
giving me permission to get messy,
to explore,
to discover not just my art
but myself.
Small things
gave me permission.
Small things sometimes
make a world of difference.

Coneflower Shadow

I stepped through the shadow
of the tall coneflower
and blocked its lines,
made a gray blob,
a me shadow,
where coneflower shade once was.
I quickly stepped out again.
The shadow swayed a little
as if to say thank you,
for she had only a few hours
to stretch herself
across the cedar-stained deck
and was already shrinking
as the sun climbed the sky.
She will wane to a nub at noon,
then lengthen
as the afternoon wears on,
until the sun sinks
and all shadows melt
into the shade of night.

Why I Need My Garden

In the window
above my kitchen sink,
one golden bloom rises on a
toothpick-thin stem
in a tiny pottery vase.
A black-eyed Susan.
I lean closer,
admire her petals,
her dark brown center.
It's like looking into the smile of God.

Outdoors, pink coneflowers sway
beside magenta coleus leaves
blanket-stitched along the edges
in bright yellow-green.
The smile of God.

Yellow gazania blooms bright,
happily resilient in the heat.
Red-purple impatiens overspread their pot,
preferring the shade.
The smile of God.

I also know the tears of God.
Anyone with eyes to see
and an open heart
feels the sadness,
knows the tears.
So many.
Too many.

That's why I need my garden—

gazania and impatiens,
cornflower and coleus,
black-eyed Susans.
They remind me
that God does smile.
They give me hope
that we, too—
all shapes, colors, and
types of us—
can flower and flourish
in beauty and peace.
If only we will.
We, too, can be the smile of God.

Why Not Love a Tree?

It was a death, I realized,
the cutting down of the tulip poplar
taller than our two-story house.
Her broad scalloped leaves were still healthy,
along with her tulip-shaped blooms
pale yellow-green
splashed with orange in the shape of hearts
that looked hand-painted
by some mischievous wood-sprite.
She still looked healthy, shady, perfect.
Except for her trunk
now leaning at an unnatural angle,
shoved askew by storm winds.
On one side, roots had pulled free
creating a lovely-looking cavern—
if you were a fairy
or a chipmunk.
But even the small cavern was not safe.
Each gust of wind
rocked its grassy root-thick roof
and threatened to fell the tree.
Where exactly would she fall?
Would she crash into the old hackberry?
Would it take her weight?
Break her fall?
Or would she end up in the driveway?
Would she clip the corner of the house?
And when?
Luckily, she stayed standing
until the tree surgeons came.
Unluckily, it was a death.
She had begun her life as a twig

carefully carried home from school
by my second-grade son on Arbor Day.
He chose her spot and planted her.
She was barely visible on the lawn
and was mowed down at least once.
Amazingly, she rooted herself and grew.
By the time my son left home,
she was a grand shade tree
a beautiful reminder
of a little boy
with big expectations.
Now, almost forty years later,
she is gone,
and I am grieving.
Part of me says she was just a tree.
Maybe I shouldn't have loved her so much.
Then I think—why not love a tree?
Or a dahlia.
Or a yard full of violets.
Why not love a sunrise,
a sunset?
Why not let the heart break
at a beauty so generous,
so fragile.

Looking at Green

"Go outside,"
my friend's therapist said.
"Go outside and look at the green."
The used heart,
the abused heart,
the wounded soul
turns inward with pain,
tunnels in,
builds a protective shell,
like a snail, hides inside.
Colors, once bright and bold,
become muted,
care full,
shrinking into shadows,
swept into shards—
but there,
still there.
"Go outside.
Go outside and look at
all the colors of green."
My friend did.
She opened the door.
Green met her there,
and she saw that green
was not just green
but elegant emerald,
warm olive,
deep forest,
soft sage,
splashy sea green,
tart apple green,
sunlit spring green,

lime,
moss,
pine,
branching out,
stretching up,
dancing in the wind,
basking on a rock,
climbing a fence,
life giving life,
simply being,
full and changing
one day at a time,
brightening,
fading,
from one green to another,
simple,
restful,
growing,
hopeful.
My friend laughs now with delight
at being precisely who she is.
She is evergreen.

Steady and Soft, Damaging and Deadly

After weeks of drought,
the rains finally came,
steady and soft.
I sat back and listened to
the soft tap of droplets
showering the windowpane,
the white noise of water boiling
in the kettle,
the gentle creak
of the rocking chair,
whispery gusts of wind,
the hum of the fridge,
the purr of the cat,
the turn of a page,
the distant whir of a jet in flight,
fading into the sound of the rain,
the delicious,
life-giving
rain.

This is not
what my friend heard
in North Carolina,
for this same storm system
that brought me sweet,
life-giving rain
wore a wild mood
when it reached her
rushing in a raging torrent,
a damaging, deadly downpour.

In my back yard,
when the rain ended,

the renewed trees dripped,
sated and peaceful.
Birds warbled and chortled,
branch to branch,
tree to tree,
a clear, world-washed song.

When the rain ended
in my friend's back yard,
trees lay uprooted,
muddy floods of river water
swirled and swallowed
tangled branches.
I have to believe that in her neighborhood,
birds still sang from the tip-top
of whatever withstood the storm—
peaked roofs,
stubbornly strong trees,
a post, a pole,
a precariously tilted sign.
May the birds always sing
their ancient wisdom,
their song of courage,
comfort,
and hope.

Look What I Found

"Yook! Yook! Yook!"
my three-year-old neighbor called
to her mother.
"Yook! I foun' a yaybug!"
I smile at her discovery
as I weed my front garden.
I'm discovering the names
of the prolific vines that climb
and twine around iris stems,
overrun dried daffodil leaves,
make their beds among soon-to-bloom daylilies.
Virginia creeper, Carolina snailseed,
Black Medick, ground ivy,
Greenbrier, stick-tights,
and wild grape vines with curly tendrils,
these vines are profuse, persistent, possessive
and would claim the entire garden
if I let them,
but I'm making way for daylilies,
surprise lilies,
allium and gladiolas.
So I trim back the vines.
Some pull straight out
in long strands.
Some I have to clip,
tugging thin stems taut until I find
the earth-end and then snip them.
Some have twined themselves
around the stem of an iris or a lily
or a curled canna leaf trying to unfurl.
These I carefully and gently unwind.
But I don't touch the clematis vine

veiling one end of the garden,
for it's Nature's bridal bouquet,
soon to bloom in a sweep of small white flowers.
Sultry sunbeams pierce through rain-heavy clouds.
The day sweats and so do I.
Clip.
Tug.
Untwine.
I find the first white clover
under the cannas.
And look! Look!
I, too, found
a ladybug!
Although now,
I think I shall forevermore
call her a
yaybug.

Until Peace Settles Deeply

A broken heart, I think,
sometimes shields itself
under the guise of anger,
resentment, and bluster.
It's easier
and maybe feels safer
to harden
instead of soften,
to shield
instead of bare itself,
to try to control
instead of letting go.
That truly may be the wise path
until wounds turn to scars,
until we stop collecting thorns to
shore up that shield
and instead
gather for ourselves the healing herbs
of goodness and mercy
until peace settles so deeply in us
that we realize
that from now on,
thorns may prick,
but only scratch-deep.
They will no longer embed themselves
as splinters in our heart.
For we know who we are—
scarred but
whole and holy.
We are those who not only
gather goodness
but give it away freely,

especially to those still collecting thorns,
still shielding their hearts.
Peace, love,
goodness and grace.
Gather and give.

Swallowing Sunshine

Today I picked three palm-sized stars
with pure white petals.
Mandevilla they're called,
a fancy name for a friendly flower that grows
on vines that twine around fences and stakes
and the gangly stems of neighboring black-eyed Susans.
In the center of each bloom
is a deep throat of golden yellow
as if it has swallowed sunshine.
They hold this inner glow of morning
through afternoon
and sunset
and twilight
and into the night.
Today I picked three palm-sized stars,
and they asked me what glowing ideas
I have swallowed.
Which are worth holding center-deep?
Which lead to peace and kindness
in this vining, entwining life?
Which will hold a warm glow within me
through sunset and twilight
and into the night?
I think I know the answer.
Only the golden grace of peace and lovingkindness
can last the day and pass through the night.
Today I picked three palm-sized stars
and, for a moment, held in my hand a hint of
nature's wisdom.

Night Has Not Fallen

It's early twilight,
that gray-blue time of evening
when the neighborhood eases into
the quieter hours of our day.
Chili is simmering on the stove,
and the table is set,
so I sit in my rocking chair
to witness the world beyond windows,
to watch the night fall.
"Fall" is a strange way to say it.
Night doesn't really fall;
it slips in,
seeps through bare, laced branches,
slowly veils the hills.
Tonight the sky is cloud-covered,
a full sweep of blue-gray
gradually growing violet in the east
as if heaven's light switch
is slowly dimming the day.
It's a peaceful drift,
moment by moment
as the sky lets go of its dusky gray
and drapes itself in deepening blue
inviting all who pause and watch
to enter its ease,
to breathe its comfort,
to settle into the serenity of evening
and experience the magic of
twilight blue turning into velvet dark,
whispering calm to a world
that will soon settle into sleep.
No, night has not fallen.
It has snuggled in.

Never Ever Before

I've always been this way, I say,
and yet,
I haven't always been this way—
not exactly,
not this unique and particular way,
living another day
with its unique and particular thoughts
and wanderings
and wishings
and astonishments.
I've not always been aware
of ideas I read
last night
sparking questions I've asked
this morning.
Each new dawn
marks a waking
to wider wondering,
deeper thinking,
and the joy of possibility.
I've always been like this.
But not precisely like this.
I've always been made new
each day.
It has always been this way.
Yet it has never ever
been this way
before.

The Key

A tiny gold plastic key
small as a thumbnail
lay under a lightpost
in a bookstore parking lot.
My grandson found it,
examined it,
wondered what it might unlock.
A fairy's door?
A toad's treasure chest?
A bird's garden gate?
Maybe.
One thing for sure:
it unlocked
his imagination.

Could it Become a Symphony?

In the branches above me,
a bird—cardinal? wren?
I'm not expert enough to say—
sings a lilting tune
and is echoed by a distant bird.
An early morning call and response.
I imagine this network of singers,
this connection between birds
who share the same song,
who hear each other
and answer
above the rush of traffic,
beyond the wind through the trees,
over the hum of the jet crossing overhead.
I imagine this stream of song
stretching like a strand of gossamer,
loose and floating but strong,
crossing the city,
one bird to another.
Could it make its way
around the world?
Could it become a symphony?
I imagine that it does.
I imagine, too, those of us
who share the same song of hope,
who protect deep peace in our hearts,
who honor loving kindness for all,
who pray for peace to blanket the world
but fear that our voices simply sound
like the thin chirps of distant birds.
Still, our gossamer thread is strong.
Does my voice echo yours, I wonder,

or is it the other way around?
As with birds,
the voice that begins the song
and the voices who carry it on
are of no consequence.
What matters is the song
making its wise way through the world
beyond the ruckus of resentment,
above the bite of arrogance.
What matters is that we never stop spreading
the possibility of peace.
Sing on, friends.
Listen to the distant voices
and the near ones,
the clarion carriers
of the call of peace.
Catch that song,
weave it into your voice,
echo its hope,
for somewhere a listening ear waits
to hear that melody,
to send it on
and on
across the world.

Silenced by the Sea in the Wind

On a windy day,
if I close my eyes and open my ears,
I can imagine that I live
beside the sea.
This sea of wind comes in waves
surging and ebbing,
a rolling surf of air
swishing through pine needles,
washing over elm leaves,
splashing on fronds of bamboo.
It's the nature of Nature
to echo herself,
the sea in the wind and the wind in the sea.
Or a bird that chirps like a yipping dog
(or perhaps it's the dog who yips like the bird).
A leaf that echoes the shape of wings,
wings that echo the shape of feathers,
feathers that echo the shape of feelers
on a fancy, flamboyant moth.
Leaves that echo the scent of lemon
or pepper
or cat pee.
But it's the sea in the sound of the wind
that silences me,
sparks my dreams,
carries me to distant shores,
to time outside of time
and leads me to suspect
that this present moment
is itself an echo
of eternity.

A Pure Stream of Blue

There's a sweet sadness,
a pure stream of blue
rippling with love and longing,
a catch in the heart,
a hitch in the breath,
hands open and empty
because of
love,
outstretched hands
palms up,
cradling sweet longing,
holding sweet space.
This is a knowing sadness,
a generous and gracious sadness,
a soft sadness,
full of memories of souls
who have flown,
a sadness relinquishing
what was never meant
to be held forever
but like a pillow
still holds the dips and curves
of one who has risen,
empty yet not empty,
traces of the one who is loved,
the sweet sadness
rippling in a pure stream of blue
that will always be.

What If?

What if you were a mouse
cornered by a cat
who only sniffed at your trembling hindquarters?
And what if this cat had fur
the soft gray color of yours?
Would you turn and take her measure—
is she likely a harmless cat
or a dangerous one—
or would you decide it wiser to run,
scurry away,
hide?
Would you escape
through the nearest dark hole
into the narrow, dim corridors
in the wall?
Would you find your way out—
out of that room,
out of that house,
never to return?
Or would you come back
after catching your breath,
just to have another look
at this much larger twin of yours?
Would you creep up
on that cat curled and sleeping?
Would you sniff her,
wake her,
make her run and hide?

The Sacrament of Waking

In the drift of easing from night dreams
into the gift of a new dawn,
there exists a pause,
a delicious time,
a handful of moments,
the day reborn in peace.
This handful of half-waking minutes
is a carrier,
a courier,
an envoy of the sacred—
a sacrament.
In the fraying fog of waking,
I feel my fragile frame,
my trusting weight generously held,
graciously cradled,
between blanket and bed,
between heaven and earth.
This moment is a silver bowl
holding silent prayers
measured in heartbeats,
whispered in slow, easy breaths.
In a handful of half-awake minutes,
time touches eternity.

Who Knew?

"There was an old woman tossed up in a basket,
Nineteen times as high as the moon;
And where she was going, I couldn't but ask it,
For in her hand she carried a broom.

"'Old woman, old woman, old woman,' said I,
O whither, O whither, O whither so high?'
'To sweep the cobwebs out of the sky!'
'Shall I go with you?' 'Aye, by and by.'"

There was a time,
years and years ago,
when an old woman swept the sky,*
when the moon was the North Wind's cookie,**
and when Mrs. Peck-Pigeon
went pecking for bread.***
Who knew that such a long ago time
would take root and grow into
a warm, spacious place-of-mind,
a pool of peace,
a cup of all-is-well within me.
Of course, out in the big, wide world,
all is not well
and was not well even then,
but my heart tiptoes back
to this landing place where I can
hold the open hand of hope,
find gentle joy,
and open again and again
the treasure box
of childhood dreams and imagining,
where all things are possible

and the currency of trade is
simple kindness.
Who knew that such a pool
of goodness and trust
would never dry up
but would be there still,
seventy years on and counting?
Who knew that it would call to me
on bright spring days,
that it would be my "land of nod"
on the darkest of nights?
Who could know?
But even now,
the moon is the North Wind's cookie,
Mrs. Peck Pigeon still peck, peck, pecks,
the old woman still sweeps the sky.
I still ask her, "Shall I go with you?"
And she still replies,
"Aye. By and by."

*nursery rhyme **Vachel Lindsay *** Eleanor Farjeon

Every Drenched Thing

Every drenched thing bows to the rain—
branches weighed down with water,
marigolds sated and soggy,
lilies drooping and dripping.
This is not a cool, crisp perk-me-up rain
but a bucket dump so heavy
that it will leave a sultry, thick wet blanket
lazing on the lawn,
steaming the garden.
As the downpour eases to a steady silver shower,
clouds drift apart,
sunlight elbows through.
I scan the sky expectantly,
hopefully…
and I am not disappointed.
Against a billowed backdrop
of blue-gray clouds,
a veil of color gently curves,
gift of rain and sun,
sign of hope,
smile of God,
heaven's arms holding space,
sharing the secret that all light holds:
a glorious variety of hues,
reminder of the glorious variety of humans,
of plants, animals,
rocks, rivers,
skies, seas.
I can't help but smile and hope,
for on the other side of the rain
there is a luminous bridge,
arcing in a joyful embrace of us all.
On the other side of the rain
is a rainbow.

A Rather Large Keepsake

The little girl is made of iron.
Stiff-backed and still she stands
holding up a garden hose to
water whatever she can—
black-eyed Susans in the fall,
coreopsis in the summer,
larkspur and salvia in springtime,
seed pods and freeze-dried leaves in winter.
Unmoving, resolved, in wind and rain,
in snow and hail and sunshine,
she keeps her vigil.
My father had her made for my mother.
They raised four daughters, and
while none of us ever stood this still,
not even playing hide and seek,
maybe this girl was a reminder
of wiggly giggly girls grown
and going their own way.
Now that both my father and mother are gone,
this little iron girl belongs to me,
a rather large keepsake,
a reminder of girls growing up
and now growing old.
But even more,
she reminds me that
we have weathered the world's wildness before,
and can again,
in every season,
persistently watering,
insistently cultivating
peace—
not without pain,

not without questions,
but also not without wonder,
not without heart.
She reminds me that
a stilled spirit,
a calm soul
is itself a keepsake
as we water
with kindness and hope
whatever we can.

Playful Day

Dawn came layered in clouds this morning,
a parfait of light and shade,
pale peach and pale blue
turning lavender as I watched.
Out of the layer of peach,
a glow brightened, bloomed,
sparkled out—
the sun bubbled up,
a happy round lemon.
Those who know,
who foretell the weather,
say that this will be our day,
an interplay of cloud and sun,
a mix of light and shade,
until the day tires of play,
leaving a mountainous cloudscape
in the west,
which will flatten, crestfallen
into a field of darkening gray.
The wind will sigh, strong and gusty,
and the playful day
will settle
into an evening
of rain.

A Silent Slant of Light

In late afternoon, that quiet artist,
the sun,
pours her light at a slant
into my sunroom—
named for her, of course.
She brightens the window shades
to an eggshell white,
glows neon pink through the translucent
pads of the Christmas cactus,
sparks the tips of my cat's fur,
gifting her with a silver halo.
Outdoors, she dapples the hackberry
with drifts of green,
lights the fiber between
thread-thin veins of fig leaves,
brightens the fountain of romaine leaves
growing in a raised bed,
edging them in white.
Across the deck, she throws shifting shadows,
creating an abstract of dark, thin stem lines,
grayed patches of leaf shade,
rounded shapes of poppy seed heads,
rippled forms of petunia, marigold, geranium.
I close my eyes and face her brilliance
as she eases lower in the sky.
Her parting kiss, warm and gentle,
paints a smooth, fire orange glow
on my closed eyelids.
The sun is wise.
She says, "Shine through where you can,
and where you can't,
stun the world with the beauty
of the shadow."

Simply to be Present

You're the strongest woman I know, she said.
But I do not feel it.
The truth is
I am not strong.
I simply put one foot in front of the other
and move forward,
rather slowly these days,
sometimes sure-footed,
but just as often stumbling.
No, I'm not strong.
I'm just here.
I'm simply present.
I shrug—I just am.
It's said that when Moses asked God's name,
God answered, "I am."
Maybe that's the strongest
anyone can be,
to simply exist
in spite of every wind that blows,
hot or cold,
gentle or fierce,
east, west, north, or south,
to take one more step
and say,
I am.
With all my quirks,
with all I know
and all I don't know,
I am.
I just
am.

The Geese Come Flying Low

The geese come flying low this morning,
two of them skimming the treetops,
their crawnky call timed with the pulse of
wingbeats:
"Look, look!
Here, here!
Now, now!"
And I do.
Gray-white bellies buoyed by the breeze,
wide wings flapping,
long dark necks stretched out straight,
they're the picture of persistence,
of determination,
of certainty.
They know where they're going—
I'm guessing the zoo,
which is not so far if you're airborne.
They will be guests
at a lucky gathering of geese on the lawn.
They'll flock and strut and lunch
and gather goose gossip
and rise as a group at sunset,
free to thread their own way
back through the sky
to where they began,
calling,
"Look, look!
Here, here!
Now, now!"
And gone.

The Salty Spray of Memory

Sometimes
all the wrong choices I've made
come at me like a returning tide.
With the force of a wall of water,
they hit me full in the face,
wave after
wave
threatening to drown me in
regret.
It's all I can do to keep my footing
on this rocky beach
and let it wash over me.
For it will wash over—
I'm familiar enough with this
edge of the ocean
to know that much.
The tide that comes in will
recede,
and I will find that I am still standing,
God only knows how,
but
drenched,
I stand in the sunlight of grace,
drip dry,
breathe the salty spray of memory
deeply in,
deeply out
until my breath comes without
hitching.
Peace returns
with the hope that
as long as I am still standing,

still breathing,
then with grace,
with peace,
with love,
I can
sometimes
turn the tide.

A Waterfall of Music

I've heard it said that
often when we think we're
hungry,
we're really just
thirsty.
On a walk this week,
I thought I was hungry for
talk radio,
hoping to find hope
somewhere in news and analysis.
But then,
sandwiched between
one segment and
the next,
came an interlude of music,
gentle piano,
a drifting melody.
I paused,
closed my eyes,
let liquid notes pour over me,
a waterfall,
a silver stream of serenity,
freshening, cooling,
full of hope.
As I opened my eyes,
I realized
I had not been hungry after all
but thirsty,
thirsty for the
soul full,
drenching,
quenching
grace
of
music.

The Invitation and Promise of Earth

When cool dawn drifts through
open windows,
when the rising sun
tips the green and golding leaves and
trickles down tree trunks
in trailing drips of light,
when honking geese
cross the fresh sky,
when asters open
and the basil releases
tiny pepper-black seeds,
when the cat no longer sprawls
but curls into a cozy pose,
I know Autumn is on the way.
I also know Summer's heat
is not done with us,
but these are hints of what's to come,
promises of cooler days ahead.
Already, the earth is offering up
her generous, ripe gifts.
Soon enough she will invite us
to settle with her
into long, fallow days
of peaceful rest,
patient renewal,
potent re-freshening.
She will invite us
to join the slow, deep
in-breath and out-breath season
of all creation
calming,
becoming serene,
being revived.

Splashes in the Birdbath

Rain has come at last,
a slow, soil-soaking rain
welcomed by wilting asters
drooping marigolds
and me.
Each droplet dimples
the water in the birdbath,
each splash makes small-bird waves
that ripple out and overlap the others.
Another ripple, unseen but real,
touches and tugs me today,
a ripple of friends
who gathered last night,
an assortment of artists
soul-touched by
the grace of nonjudgment,
the freedom to discover
the art in ourselves,
to discover ourselves in our art.
A first splash rippled out years ago,
found us, overlapped us,
sent our own ripples circling wider.

Everyone washes the world
in waves that widen and overlap.
May our waves be full of
goodness and grace
to restore,
to renew hope,
to refresh
our thirsty world.

The Color of Life

The color of life
is always changing.
When I was young—
really young—
life was gold thread
weaving through cherry red,
a skipping energy,
a dancing pulse,
an impatient foot tap.
Then it turned satin blue,
the color of Sleeping Beauty's dress,
a fantasy blue
holding the hopes and dreams
of a young girl's
stars-in-the-eyes imaginings,
sweet interpretation of
what was not so sweet
but prettily laced over
in a beautiful all's-well pattern,
a when-you-wish-upon-a-star mist
of goodness.
Then came green,
an enter-into-the-big-wide-world green,
the green of spring flowing into forest.
On the edge of life on my own,
shade and sun
and hope-dappled green.
But two steps forward,
one back,
life became brick red,
the color of building
and heavy lifting

and making sure to leave windows
to look out
and doors
to get out.
Brick by red brick built a life
until I realized
that life, for me,
isn't really building a settled place
but instead carrying what I build with me.
Life became the silvery translucent blue
of a journey and the mist ahead
with brown well-trod earth on the road
edged with grasses and wildflowers
of every color,
small, swaying,
dipping in the breeze.
Life shimmers, iridescent.
It's almost impossible to grasp a color
because it's always gently changing,
almost imperceptibly.
One moment I look and it's red with energy.
The next moment it's blue
with quiet strength and solitude,
and then it's green with growth—
even in old age, growth.
Life is a kaleidoscope
changing colors,
shifting patterns.
Sometimes I turn it,
sometimes someone else does.
Sometimes it turns itself.
and the colors reshuffle.
If you live long enough,
life is all the colors.

The Wisdom of the Ink

Aprons,
plastic tablecloth,
printer paper,
black ink,
paper towels,
wet rags,
we were ready to create,
my grandson and I.
After I gave the requisite precautions,
he dripped and dribbled
black ink on white paper
wherever he chose.
Then he tipped the paper—
gently, I cautioned again,
grandma that I am—
angled the paper one way,
then the other.
Black ink eased into flowing lines,
pooled here and there,
crept across the page
as one young boy drifted
into the fascination
of the flow of black rivers
mapping themselves into tiny streams
curving,
turning corners,
intersecting.
To no one but the ink,
he softly said,
"Time to create passages,
connect with others,
and make peace."
Amen, I thought.
May it be.

Petal by Fascinating Petal

Wisdom does not automatically
come with old age.
The young closed mind
can easily become
the old closed mind.
But I am blessed to have friends who,
as they've aged,
have opened
like roses unfolding
petal by fascinating petal,
revealing the beauty of wisdom
born of years of
patience,
pain,
experience.
The opening of the petaled heart
is a kind of letting go—
letting go of demands,
of expectations,
of self-importance,
of the arrogance of certainty—
and settling into the easy breath
of not knowing,
of receiving what is
and releasing the rosy scent of love,
and joy,
and peace
into the world.
Wisdom does not automatically come
with old age,
but old age is often where
wisdom dwells.

Singing in the Storm

A river of storm-strong air,
cool and damp,
poured through my open window
and swept across my bed
in a stream of fresh silver morning
filled with whispers of rain to come.
An innocent-looking layer of clouds
announced itself in an growling, rousing,
deep-throated drumroll of thunder
and in one delicious moment,
let loose a world-class waterfall
orchestrating a symphony of storm—
wind, thunder, rain—
a rushing cascade,
a wet, splashing tumble of spring
with surprise guest artists
singing through the storm:
a chorus of birds.
Each time rain and wind diminished,
birds crescendoed
in whistles, chirps, and chortles,
symphony of celebration,
gratitude,
sweet contentment.
If I could translate bird-speak,
I suspect I would hear them singing,
aren't you glad to be right here,
right now,
refreshed
on this splendid silver morning?
Already, my heart is singing back to them,
"Yes, beautiful symphony.
Yes.
I am."

Some Faithful Thing

On a quiet afternoon
when other sounds hush
and even the birds seem to be napping,
I sit and listen to the calm tick
of the dining room clock,
and I realize that I need
some faithful thing
to assure me,
to gentle me,
to strengthen me,
something like this steady click
that goes on measuring time
whether I hear it or not.
It's a faithful thing
like winter turning to spring,
like the sunrise in the eastern sky,
like the moon waxing and waning.
In life's uncertainty,
the scramble of tasks,
the unknown and unknowable,
I need this pause,
this listening,
this sensing and settling.
I need to know
that the moon has been crossing the heavens
since long before I was born
and will be crossing the heavens still,
long after I'm gone.
And while the clock in the dining room
may go silent some day,
for now, it too
is a faithful thing

evenly measuring time,
and I need some faithful thing—
sun, moon, wind, rain, trees,
even this clock—
I need some faithful thing
to be my gladness,
my contentment.
In the midst of all that's temporary,
I need some faithful thing
to remind me of
eternity.

The Peace of Baking Bread

Rich, yeasty, cozy, all-embracing,
the scent of fresh-baked bread
warms the kitchen,
drifts upstairs,
flows through the house,
seeps out open windows,
mingles with cool autumn air,
hitches a ride on the breeze
while indoors, its warm hug
settles me.
I have worked for this moment,
measured flour, salt, sugar,
added yeast and scalding water,
kneaded plump dough
four minutes per loaf (I bake two),
press and fold,
press and fold,
a hefty eight-minute workout
for arms and hands and fingers.
Then comes the magic.
The dough rises, doubles in size
and bakes golden brown,
fresh and fragrant.
All is well with a loaf of bread
just out of the oven.
What's better than its yeast-warm smell—
except for a bit of butter
on that first yummy bite.

Wishing I Could Fly

A V of geese, calling out,
crossed the cloud-rippled sky,
and I, below, watched them go,
wishing I could fly.
I'd go west too but visit
every garden on the way
to where the sunset colors glow
and twilight cools the day.
But this is now and that is dream.
I've been west, and I know
that here is where life hums to me;
it's where my gardens grow.
The hug-warm sun sets here as well
and paints the twilight sky.
Still, I look up and fill with dreams
when flocks of geese fly by.

Home

Home is where I return
for peace,
for contentment.
It's a real place
with an address,
an aroma,
a pillow I call mine.
And yet, deep down, I know
it's not permanent,
and if I go away
to someplace new
or old,
it can't uproot itself
and come with me.
And what if I don't make it back?
Home—it's a real place
with a real face,
but then again,
it's more than that.
It's where I go in my heart,
where I remember I'm okay,
where I settle,
at peace with memories
and hopes and dreams.
Home is wherever I am,
where I pillow myself,
where, in my heart,
I'm content.

November Marigold

It's warm for mid-November.
The lacework branches of
elm, poplar, and hackberry
still hold half their leaves,
and marigolds still bloom in the pot
beside my back door.
A bee visits the merry, gold,
peppery-sweet blossoms
and forages in the rich center of each.
I once lived in a house
where marigolds filled
the entire front garden.
On the sidewalk bordering that garden,
my first child took his first steps.
So, dear marigold,
you may always mean lunch to a bee,
but you'll always mean first steps to me.
You will always make me smile.

Life's Secret Answer

When I was younger,
I thought I had to find
all the answers.
I thought there were
answers to find.
Now that I'm older,
I'm holding the questions
and turning them over,
watching them sparkle and twinkle
and laugh,
for holding the questions
is life's secret answer.
Every day, all is new
and uncertain
and certainly mystery.
What matters is not
the answers
but the questions,
how I hold them
and lightly unfold them,
how I ask them
and listen for a hum,
a nod
a yes, this is a good question,
a mystery,
an unmapped path,
a happy chance,
a happy choice
to carry the questions,
to ponder and muse
with "perhaps" and "maybe"
and "we'll get there."
Get where?

And when?
Who knows?
Do I care?
Not really. It's more
exciting and joyful
to live in the unknown,
muse on the mystery,
cradle the questions,
and laugh out loud
at the memory
of thinking I had to
know.
No.
There's no knowing
and no joy in stopping the search,
of being so certain.
The quest and the question—
now there's the dance,
the chance,
the romance.
There's the flying,
the flow,
the soft, easy drift
of not having to know.
It's the smile of the soul
serene and settled,
the secret of being satisfied with
open windows and doors,
wind blowing thoughts around,
presenting possibilities
holding hopes lightly
and wishes wisely
and reveling in
wonder.

Risking It All

"Wage peace," she writes,
this person I do not know,
reposted by someone else,
a mere acquaintance.
"Wage peace."
I know what she means,
but my mind jumps to the minimum wage,
which does not provide much peace.
Besides, peace seems the minimum of wages due
when I sink into my pillow at the end
of a day of diligent and otherwise
unpaid work.
But that's not what this person means
when she writes, "Wage peace."
She means, of course, to counter
the waging of war, to say that
instead of engaging in war,
we must engage in peace.
But my mind jumps to
that other form of wage:
wager—a bet or a pledge.
Now the meaning splits wide open.
Pledge yourself to peace.
Bet on peace.
Risk it all
on the hope
of peace.
This, I think, is both wage and wager.
So I pass it on to friends,
to mere acquaintances,
to strangers
as we link thoughts,

hopes,
dreams,
bets.
I lean in close.
"Wage peace," I write.
"Pass it on."

The Writing Class

Listen to the stillness—
nine writers,
their thoughts full and circling
like wisps of colors—
if I could see their thoughts—
some jagged-edged,
others smooth as smoke.
Hands softly slide across paper,
catching thoughts mid-flight
turning them into ink marks.
Pens and pencils scratch,
soft and swirly,
sometimes hesitating,
other times racing
to keep captured thoughts
from escaping.
Our soundtrack comes from outside,
a muted whoosh
of cars and trucks passing.
Inside, we, too, are journeying
through voices in our minds,
through memories
and wonderings
and questions
and answers—
though at least for me,
there are more questions than answers,
and every answer brings more questions.
Now a train rumbles past,
brakes squealing,
for we're in a building by the train yard.
As the rumble fades,

quiet descends once more.
The pop of the spine of a journal,
more scratching,
a swish,
a shift,
and the quiet of nine writers
writing.

In The Realm of Inner Peace

In the realm of inner peace,
two rivers flow,
one tumbling incautiously over stones
gray with pain,
one smooth and rippling,
easing its way with glints of courage,
fresh vision,
and quenching calm.
These two rivers often run side by side,
one splashing into the other
before joining and sharing their waters.
We dip cupped hands in and drink
and bathe our spirits in both.
We laugh.
We weep.
We find our own way through the rapids
and into pools of momentary stillness
before we journey on.
For this is the way,
the path,
the course of life.
There is no map.
But listen.
Listen to the song of the waters.
Follow the flow of the two rivers.
For here in this realm,
there is inner peace,
and the table is always spread
for welcome.

Held Between

My sunroom floor turned into
a game board dotted with
grandson-made Lego creations
that moved in ways only he understood
in his game-wise mind,
ways I was trying to comprehend
when I looked out the window and saw
a chipmunk pouching sunflower seeds,
the overflow of a refilled birdfeeder.
"Look!" I pointed.
We both paused and watched,
transfixed by this small creature
busy with her daily task.
All the game tension,
the do-I-move-now and how,
ebbed away, leaving
a sense of peace.
We were silent,
entertained—
literally held between—
in a time out,
and once again, I realized:
moments of all-is-well appear
like steady stepping stones
across a rushing brook,
like restful benches
along a hiking trail.
So much peace comes from
stepping across the stones,
resting on the bench,
stopping to watch a chipmunk.
So much peace comes from the
pauses.

Feed Me

In the floral department of
my local supermarket
sat a tiny Venus flytrap,
its three leaf-mouths waiting,
open,
alluring red throats
exposed,
jaws outlined with
thorn teeth
always hungry.
The clear plastic cylinder
that held it was inked
"Feed Me."
I bought it.
Gave it to my grandson,
who was delighted.
"We just talked about these in school!"
Back home,
I sink into my easy chair,
pick up my phone,
to check the social media posts that await me,
mouths open,
alluring red throats exposed,
jaws outlined with
thorn teeth
always hungry.
"Feed me."

Center Stage

For one bright moment
before the sun set,
its spotlight fell full on
three bunches of crape myrtle blooms,
dazzling them to a deep pink blush
as they hung like fancy chandeliers
on gently arced branches
high above the shadowed lawn.
For one bright moment
they took center stage
before the sun eased its beams higher
for its last brilliant gift of the day,
leaving the pink blooms fading into
the settling peace of twilight.
As my birthday came and went this week,
I saw myself in those frilly, full,
gathered blooms,
for it seems that all of life
buds and blossoms
and opens into full bloom
for one bright moment
before the sun sets.
I am grateful to see,
in the settling twilight,
a beautiful peace.

When Dawn Raised Her Window Shade

This morning,
dawn quietly raised her window shade, releasing
a stream of gold that flowed
across angled roofs and leaf-strewn lawns.
The brilliant stream wandered west,
a glowing, growing, widening river
warmly hugging the autumn garden.
Orange peppers blushed red,
purple pansies nodded,
black-eyed Susans brightened.
A river of sun dappled fallen pinecones,
speckled spent coneflowers,
splashed up tree trunks to spotlight the elms
and burnish yellowing poplar leaves.
This was morning's golden gift
when dawn raised her window shade
and I raised mine.

The Dance of the Season

It's the dance of the season,
the frolic of Fall.
Leaves
drift
down.
Pollen freckles the birdbath,
tickles my nose—
a snappy breeze,
an autumn sneeze.
Branches bow,
a leaf breaks loose.
Then another.
And another.
Lifted and swirled,
tossed and twirled,
they join the drift,
the sink and lift on
cool currents of air
that stir them around
and down
to the ground
to scuffle and settle.
All the while, the breeze whispers to leaves
still clinging to branches,
"Come and dance.
Come and dance."
And they do,
and they will
until branches are bare
and a chill stirs the air.
Then Fall flicks her skirts
and flirts with Winter

who knows this dance well.
She'll take the lead
flinging flakes of frost
in a waltz with the wind.
But that's weeks away.
For today, it's a breeze
and a sneeze
and a timid drift
of golden leaves.

When Life Calls You Back in Time

Hello, fellow time traveler.
Where do you go in your thoughts,
in your heart
when life calls you back in time?
Skip past the sadnesses,
the fright, and the wounds.
Where is the glad,
the restful,
the peaceful place,
the day that light filled you,
the moment of smiles and laughter,
the curious discovery,
the gasp of awe,
the place of purpose?
These are the pure gold,
the charms to collect,
to string together into a necklace
or a clutch of prayer beads.
Hold onto these, fellow time traveler.
Burnish them with gratitude
until they gleam and glow,
for they will lighten the load
and brighten the way
along the path ahead.

One Raucous Love Song

When the crow calls,
my heart returns to Texas,
to the prairie where I grew up with
stubby mesquite trees,
prickly pear cactus,
crooked-limbed live oak,
swathes of yellow-green pastureland
rugged cattle,
a wide, wild sky holding
thunderheads miles high,
golden-orange-red sunsets
deepening into velvet-dark,
star studded night sky,
and wind,
always wind,
dry wind,
whistling through power lines,
whipping branches,
bending grasses,
flapping skirts and shirts,
sweeping dust from here to
who-knows-where,
feathering the feathers of the crow
who is maybe related to
the one outside my open window
now carrying me back
hundreds of miles,
dozens of years
with one raucous
love-song of a
caw.

Making Waves

I think we send out waves—
don't you?
Not the waggle of a hand
in greeting or going
but unseen waves rippling out
from us into the world.
Call them thoughts,
call them prayers,
call them hopes,
they roll out like a rhythmic tide,
heartbeats set adrift
through invisible currents
all around us to
ebb and flow,
weave and wander
around and between us,
waves of presence unseen,
unbounded
unlimited,
untamed.
Mine meet yours and mingle,
expand the dance.
May they be waves of
grace and goodness,
generosity and joy,
compassion and strength.
May we wash the weary world
with wonder.

Morning Gold, Silent as Breath

She is such an artist, the sun.
I watched her rise today,
a brilliant yellow-orange backdrop
to the dark green silhouette
of the neighbors' bamboo.
Her morning gold, silent as breath,
spreads wide,
slides between cane and leaf,
creates a shape-shifting mosaic,
light and dark,
shadow and shine.
She shoulders higher up the sky
with wise warmth,
quietly whitening thin-stretched clouds
feathered across the high, icy blue.
She is just getting started,
for the whole world is her canvas,
and she takes her time,
for she has all the time in the world.
Her fluid beauty ebbs and flows
as shade and light flirt,
drift,
slow dance,
weaving magic into the day,
sparking autumn-touched treetops
into gold and copper leaf-flames.
She is angling now to give us
her brightest and best
even as the days shorten and cool.
I will watch her paint this day.
I will watch her dance with shadow.
And maybe I, too,
will dance.

That House is Empty Now

The house is empty,
my sister texted.
The house where we grew up,
where my mom decorated
for every holiday on the calendar,
where my dad, without warning,
would break out in a random song
from his vast repertoire—
Gilbert and Sullivan, Carmen, crooner tunes,
love songs for mom even after she died.
On his own last day, from their bed in that house,
he warbled a couple of bars
of "Molly Malone"
and I finished the line,
"alive alive-oh."
That house is empty now.
Then again,
it's not.
Every room holds memories.
Every door and window,
every wall,
the fireplace, the kitchen, the back porch.
The memories don't die.
The beauty doesn't die.
The grace and generosity don't die.
In Daddy's last days,
when someone would visit,
he would say, "We had a good run, didn't we?"
Yes, Daddy, we did.
We had a good run in that house, and
oh God, how do I ever repay all the good?
The answer arrives

before I finish the question:
Embody that goodness.
Match it.
Become it.
Give it to your children and their children.
Share it with everyone you meet.
Breathe it out to the world.
For this love,
this joy,
this peace
is forever and for all.
This house will never be empty.

Hanging On

Last crisp leaf shivers
dangling in the frosty breeze.
Don't let go just yet.

Having the Maybes

I'm having the maybes today.
The longer I live,
the more maybes I have.
Maybe I will breathe easier.
Maybe my shoulders will
relax—
or my arms
or my hands,
maybe all three.
Maybe peace will come.
Maybe I'll
be still
long enough to feel it,
know it,
catch it,
carry it within me.
Maybe I'll get an insight—
or not.
Maybe I'll never be
so arrogantly sure of myself
ever again.
Maybe my heart will
re-tune itself to hum
a richer, fuller
melody.
Maybe I'll hear Life laughing
in delight
at me and my
maybes.
Is this wishful thinking?
Is it hope?
No matter.
Maybe my maybes will
come true.

Flames of Spring Green

This morning my hydrangea,
bedraggled and brown,
decided Spring has arrived.
Each spindly stem,
lined with loose withered leaves,
has become a spindly candle
topped with a tiny flame of
spring-green leaves.
I shake my head. It's December.
Doesn't Nature know better than to
leaf out
when Winter is just days away?
Nature whispers, Enjoy my candles,
my hope,
resilience,
renewal,
reawakening,
untethered to season.
Nature is budding
just for the joy of it.
Yesterday, someone asked me,
How old are you?
Seventy-one, I told him.
Really—he said—I wouldn't have guessed.
Really.
Yes, really.
But I, like my hydrangea,
have decided that Spring has come.

Winter and the Wild

On the first day of Winter,
as I pull into my driveway after dark,
my headlights startle two gray-brown rabbits
who had been sitting there in the cold—
chatting? Listening? Sniffing the air?
One bolts to the right,
the other to the left,
their white tails bobbing.
They live somewhere in my yard, I think,
perhaps snuggled under an arch of berried bushes
or tucked near the trunk of a pine,
or nestled under a thatch of twigs.
How do they survive the cold, I wonder.
They don't dig dens,
or so I've read,
for they might get trapped by a fox or coyote,
who also roam our neighborhood,
the wild living among us.
Then again, as I watch the white-rumped rabbits
bounding into the darkness,
I realize that, actually,
it is we
who live
among them.
Happy Winter, wild ones.

Lasting the Winter

Walking back to my house
from my mailbox,
I often look up
to where treetops touch the sky.
Today, I paused to count nests—
seven in different trees—
tucked high in the elbows of bare branches.
I first noticed them in the fall
when foliage thinned
and leaves fell.
So far, they've survived winter winds
and downpours of ice-chilled rain.
I've read that most birds
don't return to last season's nest.
They build fresh ones.
But I wonder if these old nests
have been a refuge for birds
caught in a cold winter drizzle.
Each seems an obvious oasis,
an inviting island under a field of clouds.
Or stars.
Or a crisp blue frosty sky.
I will not know if the birds return
to these nests,
for the trees will soon leaf out again,
and the nests will be hidden.

I think of those of us who are nesting,
holding space for family,
for friends.
In breezy, balmy seasons of life,
we're sheltered and hidden and full.

But when branches are bare
and icy winds howl,
when darkness comes early
and stays late,
it's then that we can look around and see
that we're not the only tender woven safe space.
All along, there's been another nearby,
and another,
and another.
Stay safe, nests and nesters.
Hold life and love and hope.
Stay strong through the winter winds.
Spring will come.

What the Wind Said

In my lap, the cat pricked her ears,
glanced over her shoulder
at the sound of a leading wave
of a sea of wind
splashing its way through the trees
in a gusty rush of chilled air,
a cold front—
or as we used to say in Texas,
a Blue Norther.
The cat sighed and cozied in
as if to say, "And so it starts."
And so it did.
Bits of leaves and seeds
hit the window glass,
the wind chime sang,
the warm room turned cold,
drafty,
and the Blue Norther blew.
"Watch!" its breathy whisper whirled,
"Soon you will wake up to see
roofs powdered with frost."
Years ago,
on one wall of Grandmother's kitchen
there hung a picture of a red-cheeked elf
carefully torn from a magazine—
Jack Frost waving a twig wand
working his fairy magic.
Through spring,
through summer,
through autumn he waited there
until his own happy season rolled around,
and then he reigned.

So as the cat snuggled in
and I listened to wild waves of wind,
I knew that his season had come.
And sure enough—
as Grandmother would say—
sure enough, the next morning
when I looked out my cold-paned window,
I saw the world frosted icy white,
glittering in morning sunlight,
and I knew that during the night,
Jack Frost had passed by.

Winter Evenings

On winter evenings, I sit at a window
and watch the twilight sky
as the sun slips away,
leaving in its wake
a gift of shifting color.
Tonight, the sky is soft,
a silver blue tinted with yellow,
and patches of pink.
Bare branches of backyard trees
curve and cross in silhouette,
upstretched in silent worship,
vespers on a silver evening.
Between and beyond
the filigree of twigs and branches,
a light appears,
bright white,
barely moving.
A distant plane.
Slowly,
smoothly,
quietly
it traces a line
through the delicate maze,
then glides away
as the silver blue sky,
slowly,
smoothly,
quietly
darkens
into a rich hush,
the velvet blue
of a winter night.

On Icy Tiptoe

Winter welcomes,
beckons,
invites us to
pause
on the brittle brink of the year,
witness
the shimmer of the season,
listen
for undertones of time passing
on icy tiptoe,
breathe
the crisp air.
Drink all of it.
Deeply.
Deeply grateful.

The Contours of the Seasons

Sunlight gives a brief nod
to the north of the world
this time of year
as Day is quick to pull her cloak
back around her shoulders,
to doze in darkness again.
But from this Winter Solstice moment,
each new dawn will come earlier,
each sunset will take its leave later,
light will linger a while longer,
anticipating Sunlight's reign.
All of nature—
cardinals, robins, juncos,
crickets and moths,
elms and hackberries,
even dirt and rocks—
follow the contours of the seasons,
the ebb and flow of light and dark,
the interplay of cold and warmth,
the whims of the wind,
the moods of the rain.
Darkness gives way to light,
cold eases into warmth,
wind calms,
rains soften.
Nature teaches the rhythms of life.
If I pause to feel her heartbeat,
listen to the whisper of her breath,
match my steps to her dance of Time,
then when sunlight gives a brief nod
at this dark time of year,
I smile and nod back.

Winter's Brittle Beauty

I am warm-weather at heart,
loving all things green and growing,
but when bare elms stretch
in latticework across the sky
and pine branches bow to a cold, fresh wind,
when clouds layer softly in shadowed grays,
and dried blooms and crisp leaves stand stiff as straw,
when marigold seed pods dangle on their stalks,
and basil seeds shelter on tiers of miniature pagodas,
when frost dusts shingles,
and smoke rises in lazy curls from a neighbor's chimney
and the scent of wood smoke drifts through the air,
when a chilly in-breath fills my lungs and clears my head,
then I am grateful for Winter,
for her brittle beauty,
for Nature's season of rest.
The world seems somehow simpler,
and I am simply grateful.

The Changing Weather of Peace

Peace and stillness—
sometimes they go together,
sometimes they don't.
Like wind,
peace can breeze in softly,
but it can also whistle sparkling cold
through cracks in closed hearts.
Wake up, it says, all will be well.
There's a pensive peace
that watches the sky for storm clouds.
There's peace that sighs in relief
when trouble skims past,
simply rocking branches, teasing leaves.
Then there's peace that weathers the storm
like a boulder unmoved,
the tree left standing.
And there's a festive peace,
noisy and fresh as a sudden spring shower,
full of laughter, lifted glasses, shared stories.
This holiday season held that peace for me—
a flowing, swirling, rushing peace
of listening and watching the joy of family,
the gratitude of gathering,
the hope of health and happiness to come.
Now that family has left
and I sit alone in my family room,
the stillness returns.
Peace drifts down like silent snow,
and I know that peace
is the weather
of the healing heart.

What's the Hurry?

Today's to-do list is long—
Clear the back deck of dried beans
and a drinking straw
left from yesterday when I taught
my grandson how to make
a pea shooter.
Clean the upstairs bathroom.
Vacuum.
Bake bread.
And whatever else comes up in between.
But my cat was on my lap,
curled and cozy
as if to say,
what's the hurry,
this,
this,
this is what's important.
And I noticed how brown strands of fur
mingled with gray,
how the white was growing whiter with age,
how her closed eyes smiled
and her breath gentled in and out.
I hushed the waiting tasks,
felt the warm sun on my shoulders,
listened to the quiet
for a moment
and a moment longer.
When I rose to tackle my to-do list,
my cat followed me upstairs
and sat in a splash of sun,
watching
as I calmly cleaned the bathroom
to a porcelain shine.
She was at peace.
And so was I.

Bowing Pines, Drifting Clouds, and the Scent of Rain

"Deep Peace" is a traditional Gaelic prayer that inspired me to write my own words to this brief, traditional blessing. It's my prayer for you.

Deep peace
of the bowing pines to you.
Deep peace
of the drifting clouds to you.
Deep peace
of the scent of rain to you.
Deep peace.
Deep peace.

Deep peace
of a quiet dawn to you.
Deep peace
of a blooming garden to you.
Deep peace
of the gliding geese to you.
Deep peace.
Deep peace.

Deep peace
of the dozing dog to you.
Deep peace
of the purring cat to you.
Deep peace
of a gentle hug to you.
Deep peace.
Deep peace.

Deep peace
of the evening star to you.
Deep peace
of a cool night breeze to you.
Deep peace
of a silken pillow to you.
Deep peace.
Deep peace.

Deep,
deep
peace
to you.